Surviving a Malpractice Suit

Dealing with
Litigation Stress
For
Health Care
Professionals

By
Thomas P. Cox, ARM

.

Title: Surviving a Malpractice Suit:
Dealing with litigation stress for health
care professionals

ISBN: 9781549534430

Table of Contents

Introduction

Dedication

It has been said that behind every man there is a great woman. It's usually true, and it's not just the support or love of that woman, it is her belief, her belief in him that keeps him going when all seems lost, when he may no longer believe in himself. So first, this is for Maureen.

It is also dedicated to all the great people in our health care system that I have met and worked with over the years. Have I met some clunkers? Sure, but these people would likely be clunkers regardless of their profession. The health care workers I am emphasizing get up every day and bring their amazing skill, intellect, and compassion to helping people when those people are at their weakest and most vulnerable. As our health care system continues through this time of great upheaval, the only people who don't seem to have a seat at the table are those providing the care.

So, this book is dedicated to them in the hope it helps them deal with their many challenges.

Surviving a Malpractice Suit
Introduction

The Cold Within

Six humans trapped by happenstance in bleak and bitter cold.
Each one possessed a stick of wood, or so the story's told.
Their dying fire in need of logs the first man held his back
For of the faces 'round the fire he noticed one was black.
The next man looking 'cross the way saw one not of his church
And couldn't bring himself to give the fire his stick of birch.
The third one sat in tattered clothes. he gave his coat a hitch.
Why should his log be used to warm the idle rich?
The rich man just sat back and thought of the wealth he had in store
And how to keep what he had earned from the lazy, shiftless poor.
The black man's face bespoke revenge as the fire passed from sight.
For all he saw in his stick of wood was a chance to spite the white.
The last man of this forlorn group did naught except for gain.
Giving only to those who gave was how he played the game.
Their logs now held in death's still hands, was proof of human sin.
They didn't die from the cold without; they died from the cold within.
-            James Patrick Kinney

It is a fair question to ask how I came to write this book and by what authority? How did it come into existence and why do I think sharing this information is worth a little bit of your time and money?

Let's start with the poem above. James Patrick Kinney wrote this poem about racial intolerance in the Ohio community where he lived, but of interest he had written it years before he felt compelled to share it with his community in the 1960s. It is a bit disappointing to realize that we felt as a nation we were far removed from those years, but recent events speak otherwise.

But think of the people described above. I am willing to bet these descriptions don't apply to you. Or didn't. You got where you are due, in part, to a decent I.Q. But that is only part of the story because your E.Q. may be more important than your I.Q.

If you are not familiar with Emotional Quotient, or Emotional Intelligence, there are several books on the matter and it is a bit more complicated than this one trait, but one significant trait emphasized in the original study results is: <u>A high E.Q denotes the ability to delay gratification</u>.

The original hypothesis, as espoused by Daniel Goleman in his 1995 book *"Emotional Intelligence,"* as with most psychological hypotheses, has been sliced and diced, has grown, and been elaborated on, and involves the ability to recognize both your own and others emotions, and how to react appropriately to achieve your goals, including the ability to delay gratification. And this is a big reason why you got to where you are today, a solid E.Q. which means you do not have the "cold within," you have a "fire" within you...or you did and now it is smoldering a little or maybe has gone out. It was your E.Q. that allowed you to look at the finished product you would become, observe all the obstacles in your path, and then not only still choose to set out on the journey, you completed it! You delayed gratification for as long as necessary to reach your goal!

The E.Q. was, in part, the "fire" within you, the passion to matter, to make a difference. Historically the health care professions have been considered "helping" professions. At its basic core health care is caritas; it is one human being helping another. There is scant room

9

for the "cold" to be within a person in the health care professions. Insurance, by comparison, is a business designed to turn a profit; getting those two opposed philosophies, caritas and profit, melded into one common goal of affordable health care in the U.S. not only seems impossible, it is stressful and a stress you deal with at some level each day. Stress is said to occur in layers and unless and until we get too many layers we can deal with it. For health care professionals, the current health care system is one more layer of stress.

But at one time, when you were thinking of entering one of the caring professions, the poem above was a great illustration of what you were not, of what you did not want to be. People choose to enter the health care professions because they have a **fire** within them, not a "cold" within them, a passion to matter, to perhaps change the world by changing one life at a time, to make a difference.

While this book has many objectives, there is only one real **goal** behind this book: **if you still have the fire I want you to keep it; if you are at risk of losing it, I want to reverse that trend; and, if you have lost the fire I want to rekindle it in you**. That is the goal, to get or keep the fire you once had burning inside you. This book was written to try and ensure that if you find yourself involved in litigation, the unique stress of litigation, when heaped on top of all other sources of stress you must deal with daily, it doesn't take from you the fire within and replace it with the cold within.

And please note that I am going to be talking to you personally, so this will be to **you**. You and I are going to have a conversation. We are going to have it because my eclectic background gave me insight into how litigation can severely impact **anyone** unaccustomed to it, but how it can be particularly harsh on you as a health care professional.

I was a health education teacher, and a high school and college coach. Much of what I taught was either directly or indirectly stress management and wellness. I came to understand that we live along a "**sickness-wellness continuum**" with people being sick or injured at one end of the continuum and being well at the other end. What I also came to understand is that **the health care professions can only take a person, if all goes according to plan, from being sick or injured to not being sick or injured; the health care professions cannot make someone well**. To move from being not sick or not injured to being well requires personal effort and commitment:

Wellness is uniquely and individually defined. Some say it is the ability to laugh, live and love, to live life to its fullest, or to live life as you wish to, on your terms. To love like you've never been hurt. But if you have never been hurt by love you have not lived, you have not tried very hard. And you love, or at one point did love, health care. As a former coach, I will tell you that handing out awards for participation and not keeping score in games may be good for self-esteem, but it's hell on self-image. High self-esteem and poor self-image is common in criminals, who feel entitled to anything. Developing a good **self-image** means learning that sometimes in life, despite what may be your best effort and with good intentions, you will lose. Try as you may, you will get your backside handed to you on a platter (I am cleaning this up for public consumption).

11

And, *sometimes*, if you love hard enough, you will have your heart broken. And what comes out of these "defeats," these "failures?" The realization that if the sun does not come up the next morning, it's cloudy. That's all. It means that life goes on and you will go on, wiser, stronger, *different* but better than you were before.

And that is how I want you to come out the other side of litigation if you find yourself involved in it or if you have been involved in it. Because I have told people this and I mean it very sincerely: **When I was a coach I was ALWAYS a better coach at the end of a losing season than a winning season. *Why*? Because I had to dig deeper, I had to work harder.** Dealing with litigation and the stress of litigation is very similar.

Example? One year I was asked to coach a middle school girls' basketball team. My brother (a wrestler and football player) had coached them the year before. He told me the good news was that the team had lost every game the year before; the bad news was that the best player had moved. I am not making this up.

We lost every regular season game. At the end of the season there was a tournament. All we had to do was lose one more game and the season was over. But the last week before the tournament I continued to dig deep, the girls continued to dig deep, no one had a defeatist attitude. The first round of the tournament arrived and the girls won! At a time when they could have just packed it in and finished the season, they dug deep and got the only win of their middle school basketball careers. They were so stunned they honestly did not know how to act and basically threw a party in the middle of the court, while I apologized to the opposing coach as her team stood waiting to shake hands.

But I learned a lot from that losing season and I was a better coach than I was at the beginning of the season and thereafter.

In 1984, I went to work as a Health Educator for a Health Maintenance Organization ("HMO") and if you are under the age of 30 an Accountable Care Organization is an HMO on steroids. The basic thrust of my work was teaching various aspects of wellness, which was designed to be preventive care. A large part of that work was dedicated to researching, developing, and facilitating stress management seminars for individual and corporate members of the HMO. In 1988, I went to work in training and development, and risk management, for a large medical center. As part of the training and development work I developed and facilitated stress management seminars for staff members. These two experiences caused me to develop different approaches for different audiences, one general for the HMO and one specific for different hospital departments. For example, the stress of being a dietary worker in a hospital is different from the stress of being on the nursing staff; the stress of being a nurse in a medical unit of a hospital is different from the stress of being a nurse working on the orthopedic unit.

In 1990, I went to work for a medical professional liability insurance company as a physician and hospital risk management consultant. The head of risk management for the company, Barbara, approached me about researching the issue of **litigation stress** in physicians and coming up with both a seminar and a program for dealing with it. Her request was more than professional: her husband, James, was a physician who had been named in a "shotgun" malpractice claim, a malpractice claim that essentially named every person and facility on the medical record as a defendant, and then over time sorted out who, if anyone, really belonged.

James, did not belong in the claim and he was dropped six months after it was filed. James was, in fact, told early on that he should not be in the suit and would be dropped. However, Barbara related that she essentially "lost" her husband during those six months and for a few months after he was dropped from the suit. She described this mild-mannered, even-tempered man, who loved life and his work and his patients, as turning into someone she did not recognize, someone quick to anger, frustrated, tense, and who suffered from bouts of insomnia. Someone who had previously loved his work now dreaded going to the office and battled with depression. In other words, James was having a severe emotional reaction to the litigation he was involved in, even though he was told that he would be dropped from the suit.

What would his reaction have been had he been kept in the suit? What would have happened had he been found negligent? What would the impact have been on his life, his personality, his marriage, his relationship with his sons, the practice of his profession?

This severe reaction to a law suit is known as **litigation stress** and it can happen to <u>anyone</u> who becomes a defendant in litigation. For most people, it is likely more of a concern if someone does **not** have an emotional reaction to being named in a law suit. But <u>health care providers in general</u> and doctors specifically

14

are prone to a **severe reaction**, an over-reaction, to being named in a law suit, to the point that it can become harmful and debilitating. This severe reaction is almost to be expected from a health care provider and a <u>lack</u> of reaction may be a bigger concern than this over-reaction. That may sound contradictory, but there are very good, very valid reasons for health care providers to take being named in a malpractice suit very personally and having this extreme reaction.

It is also very important to note that a health care provider must deal with the stress of a malpractice claim more than once. In Chapter 3 we will examine how having a malpractice claim can result in you having an event you will have to deal with or confront multiple times over the course of your entire career. It starts with the actual occurrence or event; sometimes a claim might surprise you, but usually you know that something is likely on the way and you may be suffering from Acute Stress Disorder until the statute of limitations expires. But from there you may have to deal with a claim, a jury trial, insurance issues, publicity, an investigation by your state medical board, a report to the National Practitioner Data Bank, and credentialing with hospitals, health systems, and payers. Unfortunately, a malpractice claim for a health care professional is rarely a "one and done" proposition.

A few years ago, I worked with a Licensed Clinical Social Worker ("LCSW") who signed on to do consulting work with the military. Normally people such as LCSWs, counselors, psychologists and the like are cautioned to not get too close to clients, but when working with the military just the **opposite** must occur: because the military are trained to internalize stress and other problems, people who work with the military on mental health issues are trained to develop a close relationship with the patient to get the patient to open up to them.

In the case of this LCSW she unfortunately had a male patient who wanted to develop too close of a relationship. When she rebuffed his advances he first reported her to the military brass, which closed the case with no finding of fault against the LCSW. Not satisfied he filed a complaint with the state board and the board, because of profound ignorance of how differently the military-style of counseling works, issued a reprimand which was placed on her license.

Due to the ignorance of the state licensing board she had to re-live the events of this "fatal attraction" multiple times. She decided to return to working with non-military once again, only to learn that the action taken by the state board rendered her uninsurable in the standard market; an insurance premium that should have been around $1500 in the standard, admitted market became a $5,000 premium in the surplus lines market. And without insurance she could not get a job.

Another example is an OB/GYN who had a difficult claim settled by the insurance company, with the consent of the physician. What was not explained to her at the time of the settlement, or what she was under too much stress to recall discussing, was all the other impacts it would have on her. Due to the size of the settlement the physician's premium more than doubled, forcing her to not only re-live the events leading to the claim and the claim process itself, and make financial adjustments to the lifestyle of her family, but it also caused her to second-guess her decision to settle. Her increase in premium also resulted in a financial impact for her practice.

Later in this book Post-Traumatic Stress Disorder ("**PTSD**") will be discussed. PTSD can result from a single traumatic event if it is **perceived** as being severely traumatic (death of a loved one, divorce, violent or sexual assault, job loss, etc.) but can also result from ongoing severe distress or even extreme eustress, or "good" stress (as evidenced by comedian Dave Chappell who fled the country after signing a huge contract for a TV show). Some experts studying PTSD opine that continual exposure to low-level, unremitting stress can bring on PTSD, while some still insist that only being involved in war can bring on PTSD. What is agreed on is that to start recovering from PTSD you need to be removed from the source of stress, the stressor. That is the "post" part of PTSD. Coming home from active duty in the Middle East is the first step in helping the military deal with PTSD. But for health care providers in litigation, the traumatic event can keep going for months or years (the average occurrence-to-settlement lag time in a medical malpractice claim, the time from when the claim is filed to when it is closed, is 4.9 years). This prevents you from getting away from the event that is causing the distress and possibly the PTSD.

Regardless of whether the trauma was a **single event** or **ongoing events**, it is difficult if not impossible to start recovering from PTSD until the source of trauma is removed. What is now becoming better understood is that the longer someone is exposed to the event causing the trauma, the more physiological changes occur in the brain,

17

changing the brain functioning and, as a result, how the body functions.

The information on PTSD makes for an interesting side note, too. So much has changed from when I started on this journey in 1990. We have been through one very hard and two very soft insurance markets (a hard market, as we experienced from 2000-2006, is a time of rising premium and tight underwriting; a soft insurance market has low pricing and easy underwriting); we have been through one cycle of physicians being bought by hospitals, the physicians coming back out, and now the physicians are either owned by hospitals again (in record numbers) or Wall Street firms have put doctors in larger and larger groups, both physicians and dentists. The hospital adventure (third time is the charm, right?) is still baffling, but the formation of large groups is supposed to result in efficiencies of scale (they usually don't) and increased reimbursement (which happens sometimes, but who gets the money?). Medical malpractice insurance companies are merging and acquiring, trying to corner markets, and eliminate competition, just as the hospitals, health care systems, and health insurance companies are trying to do. And with the mandating of electronic medical records doctors have become data entry clerks, while having to pay out increasing sums of money to keep these systems up and running, all for the benefit of the government and the health insurance companies. Those are a lot of changes in a short time. Stress involves responding to the world around you, especially to changes, and dealing with excessive stress is sometimes equated to peeling off the layers of an onion. In the paragraph above there are a lot of layers.

This is not a huge, scholarly work and that is intentional: a huge, complicated, in-depth scientific tome would be difficult to focus on and comprehend, especially if you are already dealing with litigation stress or its aftermath. The seminars I facilitate normally last for two hours; the lectures I have given on litigation stress have usually lasted for one hour. It is my intention to recreate a seminar in this book that can be easily referenced whenever a "refresher" is needed.

So how did I get to this book?

After years of working with doctors who were insurance customers I was asked to give a presentation on litigation stress by David Victor of the American Education Institute (www.aeiseminars.com). This recorded, one-hour presentation was seen internationally by physicians and dentists enrolled in the Institute's risk management programs. David was nice enough to share with me that in all the years of providing risk management education to physicians and dentists the Institute had never gotten a response like it did to my presentation.

This was followed by a physician making a special effort to track me down at a medical specialty meeting, telling me that he enjoyed all the presentations I had done for the Institute, but that the one on litigation stress was the most meaningful presentation he had ever heard. And, he told me, he wished he had been able to hear my presentation and to learn this information BEFORE he was involved in a malpractice claim, something I had been told before about the presentation.

If people who were not attending the seminar solely for premium credits from an insurance company were finding meaning in what I had to say, maybe this was information I needed to share with more people! I had seen other booklets, pamphlets, and books on litigation stress, but they seemed either overly simplistic and lacking in useful information; or, they were so weighted down with scientific information as to resemble a medical school course. Maybe what I was on to, my own personal progression, was the right combination for communicating this. In other words, I know that much of what I will be saying here has been said before, but I also know from years of teaching, coaching, and risk management work that the WAY something is said sometimes makes all the difference; and, I know from my coaching and risk management work that you cannot say something once and expect people to remember it, it must be repeated in multiple modalities. **Maybe the fact I was NOT a physician, dentist, psychologist, social worker, counselor, or the like is what made the difference?**

When I was coaching, I came across the concept of "show the whole thing, teach the parts, teach the whole thing." The concept carried over to my teaching, so "showing you the whole thing" at this point means that what we are going to is:

- Learn about what malpractice is and is not supposed to be, understand how it has evolved, and understand that malpractice and outcome are not always connected.

20

- Learn about what stress is and how the term "stress" became overused to the point of being non-descriptive, and how litigation stress differs from the normal stress we experience every day.
- Learn how and why litigation stress occurs, how it can become overwhelming, learn it is based on a multitude of factors, some of which you can control now and some of which you will need to learn how to cope with if you become involved in litigation.
- Learn what Post-Traumatic Stress Disorder ("PTSD") is and how a malpractice claim can trigger PTSD, especially in susceptible people; and, learn ways to become resilient in the face of PTSD.
- We will then delve into a multitude of stress management techniques that I will argue you should learn now, before you are involved in a malpractice claim. However, if you are already involved in a malpractice claim, if you have been involved in one in the past, or know of a colleague dealing with a malpractice claim, these are the techniques designed to get you back to the "fire" within and keep that fire burning at the right level until the end of your career.
- I will then finish off with a short epilogue that details my own personal experience with litigation stress. This occurred over 25 years after I started researching and teaching about litigation stress, yet I still handled some things very badly!

21

Finally, before we start, I need you to commit to one of the most basic premises behind stress management: **It is not the situation that is causing your distress, it is you, it is your reaction to the situation. It is your choice.**

<u>Peace is a choice: you can choose peace and you can do so now.</u>

1: What is malpractice and who is to "blame"?

Medical malpractice is rarely considered a criminal act; no one goes to jail. It is a civil wrong, a tort alleging negligence in the performance of professional services rendered. In the United States and many other countries, the only way to seek redress for an injury suffered due to the negligence (or perceived negligence) of another is through the filing of a legal claim. In his book "*Payback: The Case for Revenge*," author Thane Rosenbaum speaks to early versions of the civil legal system originally being implemented to bring some sense of order to the need for revenge, or to make things "even." He opines that this desire goes back to the earliest days of mankind, is prominent in the Old Testament, and is likely coded in our DNA. Thus, malpractice claims arise out of a desire to be made whole or to get "even."

Since the 1970s there have been three "hard" insurance markets for medical malpractice insurance in the United Sates, times where underwriting was tough and premiums were high. An increase in the frequency of losses, the severity of losses, or both precipitated the hard markets. An adage in insurance is that "premiums follow losses;" if losses go up, premiums go up, if losses either come down or if premiums catch up to losses, things calm down again.

After the last hard market from 2002 to 2006 frequency flattened out and, for brief periods, declined; severity, on the other hand, continued a 40-year trend up, but at controllable rates for now. Tort reform has caused claim frequency to drop in some states temporarily, while tort reform has been declared unconstitutional in other states. So, we are in a "soft market" as I write this, but things are getting ready to change in terms of malpractice claims and malpractice insurance.

Where do claims come from? Many people like to blame **lawyers** for malpractice claims; I don't. First, if there were no attorneys would patients stop being injured by acts of negligence? Of course not! Are there unscrupulous and unethical attorneys? Absolutely, just as there are unscrupulous and unethical physicians, dentists, accountants, investment advisors, financial planners, and any other occupation you care to name. But my experience with lawyers is finding most of those that routinely push the ethical envelope are doing corporate defense work. Why? As Willie Sutton, the bank robber, said about robbing banks, "That's where the money is!" Medical malpractice defense attorneys, on the other hand, are among some of the finest people I know. Not just as lawyers but as people.

Many like to blame **plaintiff's attorneys**; I do not. Why? Because in most cases a plaintiff attorney is working on a contingency fee basis and does not get paid unless and until a case is won, with the odds stacked against him/her. To have any chance of winning the plaintiff's attorney must know ahead of time what the chances will be of, first, overcoming all the legal hurdles that have been erected over the years by elected state officials and legal case precedent to stop the case from moving forward; getting past these obstructions is in the hands of a judge. Second, once aware of the challenges, the plaintiff's attorney must still argue the claim deserves

24

to be heard by a jury. If the plaintiff's attorney can get the trial in front of a jury, he/she then must win, must convince the jury that you were negligent in what you did or did not do. <u>Why is a jury so important?</u> Because a jury is asked to determine right and wrong, not interpret the law, and juries do a good job of this most of the time. Right and wrong, good and bad, usually do not enter the equation of a civil suit until it gets to a jury. Without glamorizing them too much, plaintiff's attorneys across the board tend to be like Don Quixote tilting at windmills, taking cases on a wing and prayer against defendants who are normally well-financed.

A plaintiff's attorney must also consider that between 95% and 98% of ALL legal actions, criminal and civil, never get to trial; they are either tossed out by the court or plea bargained (criminal) or settled (civil). The difference between a plea bargain and a civil settlement is that most settlements are confidential while most plea bargains remain a matter of public record (they are often reported on the news if the crime is heinous enough). <u>Many people, including attorneys, argue that **confidential** settlements are bad for the public and for professions</u>.

In an interview, political activist and occasional presidential candidate Ralph Nader brought out some interesting points about the foundation of our legal system and what it has devolved into. Nader discussed two of the basic private freedoms we have in America coming out of medieval England, including the freedom, if you are injured, to sue in court at a trial by jury and hold the perpetrators of your wrongful injuries accountable. Nader even founded a museum dedicated to this in his home town of Winsted, CT, the American Museum of Tort Law.

For those of you old enough to remember how Ralph Nader first made a name for himself, the answer is yes, there is a Corvair in the museum.

In the article Nader goes on to explain how insurance and tort law are intertwined, or used to be, as both should play a role in quality control, safety, and risk management. Nader cites an insurance company CEO as saying that tort law is quality control. The logic is simple: insurance companies should have a goal of reducing claims to reduce losses and increase profits, subsequently decreasing the need to exercise **our** freedom to pursue someone who injured us using tort law. This is called risk management or loss control.

However, over the decades lawyers have developed fine print contracts, including non-compete agreements, which are slowly eroding tort law. In many ways, this is what most people mean when they clamor for "tort reform," some way to decrease or eliminate the ability of an individual to pursue someone who injured them, through the court system. When people use the word "reform" they usually mean an expansion of rights, but the phrase "tort reform" means to most people finding ways to restrict rights.

Normally these attempts at reform are all aimed at individuals, at private citizens, and not corporations. Why? Private citizens don't have lobbyists! Therefore, there is a decline in medical malpractice cases and products liability cases over the last 30 years or so. For example, the most recent A.M. Best report on medical malpractice, through 2016, finds that claim frequency has remained largely flat since 2003, in some years even declining. Is that because health care providers are practicing better medicine than before? If you answer "*yes*" then by implication you are saying health care providers practiced worse medicine in the past. I don't believe that. I believe that all health care providers do the best job possible with every patient placed before them, as was mentioned when I was in front of a state committee looking at malpractice "reform."

What the A.M. Best report also noted, however, is that while claim severity has continuously increased over the last 40 years, what changed in 2016 was a jump in the number of claims that closed with payments greater than $1 million. Fewer claims, larger claim payments. And 2017 has already had some very large jury verdicts, especially in states where tort reform was ruled unconstitutional.

In the bibliography, there are some books that elaborate on these and other points that illustrate flaws that have developed in our legal system and business world over time. If you read any of them the Shakespeare quote about "First, kill all the lawyers!" may come to mind. **The goal of tort reform should be to make it quicker, easier, less expensive, more equitable, and less adversarial when someone is genuinely injured due to the negligence of another person**. This will decrease the cost of litigation, both in terms of money and distress, and lead to more consistent outcomes. But any change to the system for one specific profession would likely run up against one of the freedoms in our Constitution.

Are **patients** to blame for malpractice claims? Well, they usually are the injured parties, so yes, but often you then end up exploring the wellness of the patient: have they not taken good care of themselves, not properly managed chronic conditions, allowed themselves to deteriorate to the point where any procedure that might help them has as good a chance of harming them? Sometimes yes, also, if the patient does not comply with the treatment plan very well. But they still must find an attorney willing to take the case, as noted above, and unless the patient is extremely wealthy to start with the case will likely be taken on contingency, which brings me back to the paragraph above and why plaintiff's attorneys must be very selective in the cases they take.

In 25 years, I have seen one case that I thought was absolutely frivolous and one where the presence of money allowed the patient to keep going after a physician out of spite. In the first claim the only thing I can think of is that the plaintiff's attorney was trading on his name (he was a state senator then, in the U.S. House of Representatives, now) and/or trying to mine or develop new case law. A prisoner had been brought into an emergency room for treatment. He was shackled to a gurney. The doctor told the sheriffs that to perform a proper exam the prisoner's arms would have to be released. The sheriffs explained that this was not a good idea as this person was shackled for a very legitimate reason: he was extremely violent. The doctor then stated that he could not treat the patient unless at least one arm was released. The sheriffs relented and unshackled one arm.

Immediately the prisoner flipped sideways off the gurney and on to his feet, and started swinging his fist with the free hand and swinging the gurney around using the arm that was still shackled to it. The prisoner was eventually subdued, restrained, and re-shackled to the gurney, not surprisingly the doctor was now able to

28

perform an exam despite the shackles, but both sheriffs, the doctor, and a nurse all received minor injuries.

So, who sued for malpractice? One **sheriff** received injuries severe enough that it required time off from work and "possible" nerve damage to his arm, and the sheriff sued the doctor for unshackling the patient claiming it was malpractice because the doctor "should have known better." This claim was filed, the defense immediately moved for dismissal, and the court granted it at the first and only hearing.

What about the revenge case? This involved a woman in her mid-20s who was having a series of mini-strokes. Her husband was an executive with a pharmaceutical company, well off enough that his wife did not have to work and she played on one of the United States Tennis Association teams at the country club they belonged to. My doctor was the neurologist trying to diagnose and treat the mini-strokes. He recommended she cease taking birth control pills and use another form of contraception, along with quitting smoking. The mini-strokes ceased! Without communicating with her physician, the woman started taking birth control pills again and the mini-strokes started again. Ignorant about the birth control pills and unable to determine the cause, the local neurologist referred her to a "stroke guru" at a university medical center in an adjoining state. This physician, too, was unable to find anything definitive, but did learn that the patient had started taking birth control pills again and directed her to stop.

As the patient and her husband were driving home from the university visit, in fact just around the time they crossed the state line, the patient had a severe stroke that

29

.

left her hospitalized for some time and with some deficits on her non-dominant side that improved over time. She sued the local neurologist for failure to properly diagnose and treat her, using the stroke and its aftermath as her evidence. Twice the case went to a jury and twice the jury could not reach a verdict. One complicating factor, of course was the issue of the birth control pills and contributory negligence, weighed against an apparently healthy young woman having a bad outcome.

Despite two hung juries the patient filed suit a third time with a third attorney and, for the third time, the case went to a jury trial. The night before the trial both sides inadvertently ended up in the same restaurant and the patient ended up in the women's restroom with the wife of the neurologist. The patient looked at the physician's wife and told her that they were going to keep going after her husband until they won, just so they could prove he was a bad doctor.

When the physician was informed of this and pondered it overnight, and with the specter of a third trial about to begin, the physician agreed to settle the case. I am glad to report that this case happened in 1997 and the physician retired in 2015, so he could and did move on. I am less glad to report that the patient and her husband moved to the suburbs of a large city where they lived in a gated community and the woman once again played tennis at the country club they belonged to, after hounding my doctor for over five years.

Egregious examples? Yes, but those are the only two I can think of over a 25-year career that were that extreme; in all other cases, there were people with legitimate injuries that may or may not have been caused by a medical professional, and may or may not have occurred because the care rendered was below the acceptable "standard of care" (more on this later).

How about **society**? Is it to blame? Do we have a "lottery" mentality? Well, I know a lot of doctors who buy lottery tickets, so we need to be careful with our phrasing. But while large jury verdicts get a lot of attention they remain the exception in most jurisdictions. And as will be noted a couple of times throughout this book, all medical malpractice insurance companies claim to "win" between 80% and 90% of all claims (keep in mind this includes all the cases that get thrown out before trial) and most insurance companies claim to win around 80% of jury trials (which shows you both the ability of juries to "get it right" and the respect people still have for health care professionals in general).

Given those numbers I think it's safe to say that everyone would like to genuinely win the lottery, but no one wants to "win" based on having suffered some sort of serious injury or medical error. And while states can enact tort reform they cannot ban people from seeking compensation they may rightfully be entitled to due to an injury caused by someone else.

How about **modern medicine**? Has medicine brought this on itself with its growing number of success stories that used to be failures, the increase in specialists and technology, and the outcomes it sometimes can produce? I will say that when I first started researching this subject years ago, it bothered me that essentially all medical shows on television seemed to have successful conclusions, with everything all tied up in a neat bow within 60 minutes. I am glad today to see medical shows on television that are more attuned to real life, where sometimes there is little or nothing medicine can do, where sometimes bad things happen to good people. I have personally moved past the story of Job in the last few years and find myself wondering why good things happen to bad people!

But the fact remains that the public has high expectations from our healthcare delivery system, despite our middle-of-the-road results when compared globally (a whole other book in the waiting!).

How about the **increase in specialization** from the days of "Marcus Welby, M.D." (you younger folks will have to look that one up)? Specialization does lead to better diagnosis and treatment, and usually better outcomes, but that also raises expectations. More so, the movement between providers can decrease and complicate communication and create unrealistic expectations, while increasing the cost of care. Specialists also provide more episodic care and, thus, form less strong emotional bonds with patients. Add to all the above the increasing demands placed on the health care system by government and payers, along with the rapidly expanding knowledge base due to research, the use of computers, the mapping of the human genome and many more advances, and when it comes to malpractice claims you end up looking at the one person who is always central to the care, treatment, and the outcome, be it good or bad: **you.** The one constant is you.

But why do some doctors get sued more than others? Why are there articles written about how two percent of doctors cause 80% of claims? Is this true and accurate? I have also read that 50% of all doctors will get sued at least once. Is this true? Is it competence? Is it bedside manner? Is it communication skills? Is it helping patients set realistic expectations? Why is it that to this day the largest single underwriting predictor of a future malpractice claim is a prior malpractice claim? Could it be a complicating factor from the initial malpractice claim, the litigation stress? And what of the studies that have been done, the closed medical record studies, that show that for any one malpractice case there are between eight and ten cases of documented mistakes or sub-standard care where no malpractice claim was ever filed? Could there realistically be many more legitimate malpractice claims filed?

In conclusion, it would be nice if we could pinpoint one or two things that, with tweaking, would eliminate the need for malpractice claims to be filed but that is not reality. As with any profession, as with any human being, mistakes occur and a claim, legitimate or otherwise, often follows. As will be mentioned a few times, the difference with health care is that the mistake often leaves someone **harmed physically**, sometimes for life; the challenge is determining if the harm was due to the care rendered and if that care was substandard.

Prevention

Are there things you can do to reduce the chances of being named in a malpractice claim? Yes. You have probably heard them many times over the years, in school, in training, in residency, at risk management seminars. If the following are reminders, good: one risk management technique that is often overlooked is repetition, to constantly drip information on someone and

33

not say it once and assume it will stick forever. If you have not heard some of these things, and given the way residency programs are run today with less hands-on care and increased use of testing and technology, you may not have heard these things, you heard them here first.

Risk Avoidance

I have been asked what can be done to guarantee you will not be sued for malpractice. The answer: sell suntan lotion on the beach. Risk avoidance is a risk management term that basically means you have assessed the probability of risk as being too great for you to undertake, so you do not take the risk. That is certainly a choice you can make, but not a prevention technique.

Informed Consent

Historically doctors have tended to look at informed consent as getting the "permission" of the patient for treatment. While that is accurate it understates the true concept of what informed consent should be.

I have found a lot of doctors take to this concept better when they view it as "informed decision-making." This moves the thought process from getting the permission of the patient to getting the patient to collaborate with you and help both of you, hopefully, reach the same decision as to the treatment plan. This involves you educating the patient about the condition, the treatment options, the risks and benefits of each, and the risks and benefits of doing nothing. For most conditions, this is a short process; for something complicated, such as cancer,

34

diabetes, leukemia, high blood pressure and the like, the options get more complicated as will the discussions and the decision-making process.

Two things to consider are delegating this task, which can be time consuming, and refusing to treat a patient. The process of obtaining informed consent can be delegated and multiple modalities used to explain options, but at the end of the process it is you who will be held responsible, so you must make sure the patient understands everything that was said and is clear on the choice that has been made. A recent court decision stated it is the responsibility of the doctor, but check state laws and case decisions where you practice. Frequently having the patient explain things in his/her own words is the best way to confirm consent, and OF COURSE you will document this process!

But what if, despite your best efforts or the best efforts of you and your team, the patient chooses a path that you just do not agree with or feel may put you in more jeopardy because it puts the patient in more jeopardy? Do you still have to treat the patient? **No**. With guidance from the claims person or risk manager at your malpractice insurance company, to both tap into their experience and to make sure you don't do something to jeopardize your coverage, explain in human terms why you feel the patient needs to seek an opinion from another doctor as you do not agree with the patient's choice, help the patient find another doctor, and move on. But don't be surprised if the patient comes back with a different attitude, ready to explore other options because the other doctors took the same approach you did. One of the more interesting experiences I have had in life was when I disagreed with a physician's treatment plan, so he dictated my informed refusal while I was standing in the exam room with him. It was intimidating, but after some reflection I considered it very effective. Also, he was right and I was wrong.

But don't let the patient drive the care. The worst-case scenario for letting the patient drive the care ends with a bad outcome occurring, you end up with a claim, it ends up in front of a jury. What does the jury see? The plaintiff will try to portray you as someone who let the patient decide on care and how dumb can that be?

"MDiety Syndrome"

There are people who will look at you as a god, that only a god can be so smart and learned and compassionate and caring. It's one reason people who are long-term patients of doctors often develop attachments to them.

I hate to be the one to burst anyone's bubble, but you're not a god and especially not God. You are a human being. Human beings make mistakes. If you make one you will learn from it and move on. That is how you are trained: learn from the present and move on to what is next, don't dwell on the past. One of the purposes of this book is to help you move on and continue practicing.

At the same time, many doctors resist good informed consent or informed decision-making because they DO view their decisions as being precise, perfect, above reproach and they do not want or feel the patient is entitled to have any input into what is going to be done to the patient's body or what the condition is. You will look at the medical aspects of "your" case and perhaps forget

36

there is a patient involved; attorneys are guilty of this, too, as they speak of "their litigation" as though the client is but a prop. This is not only poor practice, it sets you up for a bigger fall and a more difficult time if you have a poor outcome that leads to a malpractice claim. After all, how can "God" be sued? "God" does not make mistakes, right?

I have a theory that I have put forth and have had people ponder, and many think I may be right. If someone wants to give me $1 million to prove it or disprove it, I am open. I have a theory that doctors who come from families of doctors are more likely to be sued than doctors who are first generation doctors. Why? My theory is one of an attitude that sets the doctor up for a mistake and an inappropriate reaction to the mistake if it occurs.

Therefore, I purposely mentioned in the introduction how I ended up performing this research, developing the seminars and the program, and now writing this book. James, the ophthalmologist, did not come from a family of physicians. He had a father who was a milkman. For those of you under 30 there was a time when milk was delivered to your home in glass bottles, two or three times per week...sort of like an early version of Amazon, I guess.

Voluntarily restoring losses

Your first reaction is likely "*Isn't this admitting guilt?*" Yes and no. First, from a risk management (and human) perspective restoring losses is called "mitigating harm" or "mitigating loss." If a person feels he/she has been treated fairly, without you admitting any wrongdoing, they are less likely to file a claim. In addition, from a purely

37

legal perspective, if the person has not suffered any financial loss or very little financial loss, they have less footing on which to file a claim. One key issue for the filing of any civil claim is damages; no or little financial loss means little in the way of damages.

Therefore, most professional liability policies have "medical defense" coverage or "medical payment" coverage; you should also find this on your commercial general liability package policy. It can, under certain circumstances, allow you to pay for any medical treatment a patient receives as part of your insurance policy and it is not reportable to the National Practitioner Data Bank.

Finally, when a patient is injured the human reaction is to console, commiserate, to say "I am sorry." Is this, too, admitting guilt? In can be argued that it is, which has placed doctors in difficult positions, where the doctor would like to say, "I am sorry…" but is afraid to do so. Because of this, many states have enacted "I am sorry" laws which prohibit an apology from being used against a doctor in any resultant litigation.

However, the line you will be walking is one of restoring losses or apologizing without admitting guilt, apologizing without confessing, and for this you need the guidance of your malpractice insurance company and any attorney they may assign to work with you. As noted previously, never undertake actions that may jeopardize the ability of your insurance company to defend a claim as you may end up without insurance. Insurance companies and the attorneys they use routinely guide health care providers through these issues, so lean on their experience and expertise to help deter a possible claim and, at the same time, not do anything that causes you to lose insurance coverage.

Sound policies and procedures

Another way to look at policies and procedures is under the legal and insurance term "vicarious liability" or as I like to refer to it, being the "Captain of the Ship." First, do not confuse my use of "Captain of the Ship" with the legal doctrine of Captain of the Ship, even though they are similar. The legal doctrine, recognized in some states and not others, is that a surgeon is the Captain of the Ship in the operating room, regardless of whether the other people in the OR are employees of the surgeon or not. Thus, the surgeon is responsible for anything that happens in the OR, regardless of whether the person is an employee of the physician, the hospital, or an anesthesia group.

When I refer to being the "Captain of the Ship" I mean that through vicarious liability you will be liable for the acts of your employees, so if you are liable you should be in charge. But this does not mean that you must **do** everything, just as the captain of a ship does not do everything. What the captain of a ship does is determine what should be done, when, how, and by whom, delegating when comfortable, and everything is written down so it can be checked, followed-up on, verified, tested. These are your policies and procedures.

You don't have to **do** everything, you just need to determine what is being done and by whom, that they are competent to perform these tasks, and that routine checks are in place to make sure all is well. And, this can be delegated to various people within the organization.

Taking the time to do this will decrease the chance of errors occurring and present a solid defense to a plaintiff's attorney and jury that the practice runs a tight ship. In addition, it will be empowering your staff to contribute. There is an adage that the person who will be doing the filing (I know, what's filing?) should be the person who sets up the filing system. Likewise, have staff set up policies and procedures for their areas of responsibility so they will have ownership and get the "big picture." You will review and revise as necessary, of course, before signing off.

<u>Documentation</u>

It is likely that you have been told repeatedly that if something is not documented it was not done. Yes and no. If you give someone the wrong blood type or a contraindicated medication and don't document it, was it not done? Of course, it was.

The challenge with documentation is that it originated as a note from you to you about what happened during the patient's last visit and any carryover from previous visits. Then staff notes were added. Then the record became the foundation for your billing and reimbursement. Then it became a legal document. Finally, today the record has become computerized for most practices, based on government mandates.

I am sure there are some good things to come out of electronic medical records, but I believe they are overwhelmed by the negative things. Remember that computers were developed to store data, then sort it. What this means is that the government and private payers want **you** to use an electronic record to make **their** jobs easier, to compile data on "best practices" if these can ever truly be developed, to compile data on outliers and over-billing (or is it really under-coding?), but at the end of the day what does this have to do with improving the care of the patient sitting across from you right this minute? Likely not much.

As the late Yogi Berra was once quoted, "*You could look it up*!" I was asked to do a presentation on doctor-patient communication for the American Education Institute. I began researching the "latest" information on the subject and determined that I could **basically** use the same presentation I developed in 1992, I just had to stick a keyboard or tablet between the doctor and the patient. So, whereas doctors tended to not be great listeners in the past, on average interrupting the patient 15 seconds into the patient answering the question "*What brings you in today*?", you now had a computer further distracting the doctor, with drop down boxes telling the doctor what question to ask next, rather than the doctor listening to the patient and thinking. And this is solely about patient care; ignore for now the issue of cost, of upgrades, of training and re-training, of hiring scribes. Ignore for now the issue of hacking, viruses, worms, ransomware, and power outages. One practice I work with had its computers so severely hacked and attacked they could not use the electronic medical record for two weeks; what about lost productivity during that time and the cost of a forensic rebuild of the data?

Remember in the 1990s when any list of jobs of the future included the job "data entry clerk?" Little did we know that the "Internet of Things" would turn us all into data entry clerks!

But you need to document. You need to document to get paid and you need to document so you have a history for the patient. You also need to share this history with other providers, and staff members need to document, too. The biggest weak points? Historically it has been phone calls and medication refills. Today you have to also remember your "data trail. In the Epilogue, I will discuss a law suit I was personally involved in. Leverage in the case turned on a metadata search of my personal computer and my cell phone. Essentially every email, text, and phone call I made was "photographed" from my hard drive and my phone, documents printed, and the attorneys then fought over what was relevant (hardly any of it) and what was not.

The key point for you to remember is that you do not want to discuss the <u>details</u> of this case with anyone outside of your attorney, the claims manager from your insurance company, and anyone designated by your attorney, thereby giving confidentiality to the discussion. You may think the is overkill or an exaggeration, but do not start discussing the case via text or email with someone you think will not be involved in the case or someone you do not intend to call as a witness. If you start an email conversation about the details of the case with a family member or med school classmate on the other side of the country (or even the world, today) there is a good chance the plaintiff will request a metadata search of all electronic devices and you may end up inadvertently pulling someone into the case that you did not intend to, or weakening your case with some offhand comments. Normally the courts do not favor metadata searches except in criminal cases and want them done at or near the time of the event; as you will see in the Epilogue, this is not always the case. When a metadata search is conducted is up to the ethics of the attorney requesting it and the discretion of the court. This may vary based on your jurisdiction.

When I managed claims, I had a case that we decided to defend based on contributory negligence. We were in a state with an absolute contributory negligence law, where any patient negligence occurring contemporaneously with the treatment is supposed to ban any recovery. Some states have what is called "comparative contributory negligence," which means that if the patient's behavior is found, for example, to have contributed 50% to the bad outcome, the doctor is only responsible for paying 50% of any settlement or verdict.

We decided to try the case on the contributory negligence defense because the doctor and his staff reported that after surgery the patient was not staying off his leg, was not keeping it elevated, was walking on the cast, was essentially doing everything he was not supposed to do. The practice claimed it knew this because the patient's wife and mother both called the office asking for help in getting the patient to follow orders and, on post-op visits, the patient said he was not 100% compliant. When the patient ended up having a below-the-knee amputation he filed a malpractice suit and we defended, rather than settle, based on his contributory negligence.

We lost. Why? The staff did not document the phone calls, either from the wife or mother, or to them or to the patient, and the doctor's notes were not as firm as they should have been (according to the jury). Remember that a record created at or near the time of an event takes precedent over everyone's memory; if there is no written record a jury tends to give more weight to the patient's version of events because the patient has only seen a few doctors while doctors see hundreds, even thousands of patients. So, the patient's contributory negligence not only contributed to the bad outcome, it was likely 100% the cause of the bad outcome. Lack of documentation caused the jury to view our version of events as self-serving.

In short, all the historical reasons for good documentation remain, along with all the new demands.

Good Faith Medicine

I have stated a few times that juries usually do a good job of getting to the correct verdict, even if they don't understand all the treatment involved or the scientific jargon. One thing juries understand quite well, and that can greatly influence jury verdicts, is Good Faith Medicine.

What I mean by this is can you, through documentation and verbal recounting of events, demonstrate to the jury that you tried to do everything that was reasonable and prudent (NOTE: reasonable and prudent, not heroic) to help the patient? While juries can sometimes get lost in scientific jargon, juries can usually pinpoint it if you really did not give the patient your best effort.

And this is a growing sore point with doctors as hospitals and health systems, along with payers and demands from ACO networks, sometimes force doctors to make a choice between what demands are being placed on them from above v. what is in the best interest of the patient, just as managed care did in the mid-1990s. But if you keep up-to-date on your specialty, practice the Golden Rule, have solid policies and procedures, take steps to mitigate damages if harm occurs and mitigation is possible, and document, document, document, it is easy to prove you acted in the best interest of the patient.

The 12 Rs of Malpractice Prevention

Several years ago, I happened on a list prepared by The American Society of Internal Medicine. They surveyed their members who had been in practice for more than 20 years and never had a malpractice claim. Did they have any "secrets?"

Not exactly secrets, but it turned out they all had 12 things in common that they tried to achieve with each patient visit and insisted their staff do so as well:

1. Rapport: Good, thorough communication between you and the patient, between you and the patient's family, and between your staff and the patient. Normally friends don't sue friends.
2. Rationale: In brief, the law says a physician must use all available and relevant information to reach a diagnosis and formulate appropriate treatment; in litigation, you will be asked what you were doing and why.
3. Records: Documentation is put on trial as much as anything else and it is also used to illustrate conditions in the practice and the care that was rendered, i.e., sloppy records mean sloppy care, good records mean good care. Fair? Not always, but now you know.

4. Remarks: Harshness, excessive criticism, profanity, tirades, negative attitudes, all of these can undermine the best efforts of you and your staff, and trigger a law suit.

5. Rx's: Poor prescription practices can lead to serious trouble and this issue has become more complicated with time, additional research, discovered complications, and a continuous stream of new medications. Document a detailed history of all allergies, date your information, and display it in a prominent location in or on the paper record or constantly visible on the electronic record. And be clear with instructions, meeting the needs of the patient who quite likely knows less than you do. For example, a Hispanic patient was given medication for high blood pressure that was to be taken one tablet daily. The pharmacist wrote on the label "*Take once daily*." In Spanish "once" means eleven! A timely trip to the emergency room saved this patient from an unintended, but serious, mistake with a prescription. Not a problem anymore? As I write this I am on a prescription that advises me to place this medication in my eye "once daily." When I received the medication, I related my HBP story to both the pharmacist and the physician, neither of whom had ever taken that into consideration before.

6. Res ipsa loquitur: "The thing (act) speaks for itself." Essentially this is a legal term but to you it

means to make an honest and direct response if negligence has occurred or a standard of care violated.

7. Respect: Many malpractice suits are a combination of the patient perceiving both a bad outcome and disrespect from you and your staff. You are seeing people at their worst; a professional, human, concerned attitude can wash away a lot of anger.

8. Results: Be certain the patient knows all options before proceeding. Informed consent or informed decision-making, along with informed refusal, are phrases most frequently used, but as mentioned previously if you think of it as helping the patient make an informed decision it changes YOUR attitude.

9. Risks: Risks must also be discussed with the patients as part of the consent process. This is always a hot topic for discussion and it requires you to consider the entirety of the patient's condition and history, but discussing the rare but most serious risks and the most frequent but minor risks should help the patient decide.

10. Review: If there is a bad outcome, review the case objectively to learn from it.

11. Report: Prompt reporting of incidents to hospital risk managers or to your malpractice insurance agent or company, as well as any threatened claims, cannot be overemphasized.

12. Responsibility: Maintain all obligations in their proper focus. As one doctor opined, it is OK for the patient to act like a jerk: he is sick and that is why he is here to see us. A patient seeks high quality care, continuing medical education on your part, openness and honesty, informed decision-making, protecting confidentiality, containing costs, and disclosing conflicts of interest. An additional responsibility? Your own well-being.

What precipitates a claim?

It is easy to answer this question with "a bad outcome," but it is not quite that simple. First, there are, quite honestly, doctors who have bad outcomes and never have a claim, and there are doctors who have claims that never should have been filed. So, a bad outcome by itself is not a perfect predictor.

A little more accurate is "an **unexpected** bad outcome." This goes back to informed consent and informed decision-making, mitigation, good doctor-patient communication, sound policies and procedures, etc. All the things mentioned above designed to prevent an unexpected bad outcome from occurring.

This includes proper selection of patients. I know, the patients come to you and you see them, but you don't need to see every patient or continue every relationship. I worked with a surgeon who had been practicing for many years with zero claims, then had six in one year. It took a while to flesh this out, but the reason for the increase in claims was that the surgeon was taking on cases that other surgeons had declined. For the most humanitarian of reasons he wanted to try and help those patients that

48

no one else felt they could help. Sometimes he could help or if he was not able to help, the patient understood (get a patient's expectations in line!) but on six occasions the patients no one else would take a chance on could not be helped by this surgeon either, but in their minds, they believed he was going to fix their problems. The one challenge we had with these cases was that the defense experts had no criticism of the surgeon's technique in each case, but had a hard time defending the surgeon taking on the patient in the first place.

A trickier situation, that speaks to mitigation, is an unexpected large bill. Health insurance has not only become more complex but costlier for the patient, even with insurance. According to most studies the leading cause of bankruptcy in the United States is a large, unexpected medical bill (followed by substance abuse or addiction by a person, a spouse, child, or significant other). Health-care induced bankruptcies have decreased considerably under the Affordable Care Act, but these bankruptcies still occur today, even for people with insurance, as deductibles today can run to $10,000 or more for people who are living paycheck-to-paycheck.

For perspective, I was talking with the Chief Medical Officer of a large health system that I thought was a well-run operation. I told him I was surprised to read, in an article on struggling health systems and hospitals, that his health system was struggling and laying off people. His answer was most instructive. He said that when you compared revenue year-over-year the Medicare reimbursement was pretty much unchanged, the Medicaid reimbursement was pretty much unchanged (in the two states in which they operated the Medicaid expansion under the ACA was not approved), and the charity care was pretty much unchanged. Where the system was getting killed financially was from those people with employer-sponsored health plans with high deductibles. A visit to your office, with a deductible payment to you of $150 was OK; three days in the hospital, with a bill approaching $10,000, was just impossible for the average family. This doctor said that the only happy person in his neighborhood was someone who owned a bill collection agency!

So, if someone has a bad outcome or an unexpected bad outcome, followed by an unexpected large bill, the fuse has been lit! This is where any combination of efforts to reduce the bill or write it off, to mitigate harm, can ward off a malpractice claim. But as noted earlier, do this under the supervision of your malpractice insurance company.

Finally, relationships. We have so many different types of relationships, some we want, some we don't. Once we have them, what do we do with them? In this case, you not only have your relationship with the patient to consider, but the relationship of your staff with the patient and everyone's relationship with the patient's family, if necessary. I have seen more than one wrongful death suit filed by the family member who did NOT get to the bedside in time and was unable to say goodbye. The irony is that often that person is the last to arrive because the relationship with the patient has not been good and they wanted to "make things right" but were deprived of the chance because of **you**…in their minds. Usually these claims don't go very far, but it is one more source of stress, the treatment of the patient, the loss of the patient, followed by a lawsuit from a family member.

But I hope the message is received here. <u>There is a reason some physicians seem to never get sued despite</u> bad outcomes and unexpected bad outcomes and large bills and a multitude of reasons, and it may be simply that old standby of "good bedside manner." And if you are not the kind of person who is good at developing these relationships, in fact believe (and rightly so, to some extent) that a doctor should keep an emotional distance from your patients, then look for **staff members** who can form these strong bonds and develop these good relationships for you.

There is an adage that "friends don't sue friends" and that is largely true. But I do know of one case where the spouse of a friend sued a friend. In this one claim the doctor and patient were fishing buddies who spent many weekends on the lake. When the patient died of a heart attack shortly after his annual physical the wife sued for malpractice.   In discovery, it came out she deeply resented all those lost weekends when her husband was off fishing!

2. Stress and Litigation Stress

Stress itself is normal, but the word is often misused. Too much stress, what is called distress, is an over-reaction and it is <u>normally</u> caused by either not being in control or perceiving that you are not in control of situations or events. It is first emotional, then physical: the stressor is perceived, stress erupts, and the "fight or flight" mechanism kicks in. This is the same mechanism that kept our ancient ancestors alive, the ability to deal with their sources of stress by either fighting or running away to fight another day. Health care providers in general and doctors specifically are used to being in control. So, the intention of my work on this topic has been to help health care professionals <u>understand</u> the stressor that is causing their distress, understand why they are prone to an over-reaction to litigation, and give them the tools necessary to help deal with the distress, litigation and otherwise, until control can be regained or the source of stress eliminated.

Most of the stress research and education that has evolved over the last 80 years or so can be traced back to Hans Selye, often recognized as the "Father" of modern stress research. Selye, a Canadian physician who died in 1982, first worked the concept of stress into medical terminology in 1936. An internist and endocrinologist by training and education, Selye developed what were then revolutionary theories on the role of organic responses to emotion, illness, and injury which changed our understanding of the causes and mechanisms of disease, especially the concept that there is not a mind <u>and</u> a body, but a **mind-body** that are one, something we take for granted today.

Let's start with the "whole" again and then teach the pieces:

- **General Adaption Syndrome** ("GAS"): A set of physiological responses that include swelling of the adrenal cortex, atrophy of the thymus, the massive release of corticosteroids, and potentially gastric and duodenal ulcers. Blood flow to skeletal, voluntary muscles is increased while blood flow to internal organs and muscles is decreased, in preparation for the body to fight or run away from the source of a perceived stressor.

- **Stress:** Quite simply stress is reacting to the world around you, the "fight or flight" mechanism that has been a part of our DNA for thousands of years.

- **Stressor:** An event that causes you to have a stress response.

- **Distress:** This is a severe form of stress, either a severe reaction, such as litigation stress, or a source of stress that is prolonged and becomes debilitating, eventually leading to physiologic changes in both the brain and the body.

- **Eustress:** This is a "good" form of stress. It is the same initial physiological response, but short-lived and used to heighten awareness, response, and performance.

Selye initially defined what he observed as the General Adaption Syndrome ("GAS"), the non-specific

53

response of the body to any demand for change. In one respect, this is simply responding to the world around you and, in general, this is healthy. Arguably the only people with zero stress are dead people and people who are so mentally ill that they are unresponsive to the world around them. Viewed differently, however, it means that everything bothers us; the question is to what degree?

In his research Selye observed that laboratory animals, when subjected to various noxious physical and emotional stimuli, exhibited the same pathologic changes regardless of the stimuli. This included stomach ulcerations, shrinkage of lymph tissue, enlargement of the adrenal cortex, and atrophy of the thymus. He later demonstrated that such exposure on an **ongoing** basis could cause these animals to develop various diseases like those seen in humans, such as heart attacks, stroke, kidney disease, and rheumatoid arthritis.

Paired with his observations that people with different diseases exhibit similar symptoms resulted in Selye describing the effects of the "noxious agents" as "stress." Over time Selye's original definition got lost as the term "stress" was used to refer to any negative or unpleasant situation and was used to explain chest pain, heartburn, headache, chest palpitations, or the result of ongoing stress being blamed for heart attacks and ulcers.

As he became aware of the confusion surrounding the word "stress" and how it had become removed from his original research, Selye coined the term "stressor" to distinguish stimulus ("stressor") from response ("stress"); **thus, the adage that it is not what is happening to you but your response that matters and you can change your response**. But further refinement was necessary as it became apparent that there were beneficial aspects to stress, that it was, in fact, a remnant of our prehistoric ancestors and their need to "fight or flee" when faced with the dangers they commonly dealt with as part of a daily struggle to survive.

Put another way, much has been written about Type A and Type B personalities, the Type A being the high energy, constant motion person. In the beginning, stress management initiatives were aimed at turning Type A personalities into Type B personalities, more laid back and calm. It turned out that trying to turn a Type A into a Type B was the equivalent of shackling a race horse to a plow; it was more stressful for the Type A to try and become a Type B, so now the aim is to reduce the harmful effects of the Type A personality.

Over time the concept was further refined to include the concepts of "distress," or bad stress, and "eustress," or good stress. Distress is what most of us think of when we hear the word stress, the hypothalamic – pituitary - adrenal axis which is the mechanism by which the body copes with stress, a reaction to something that leaves us afraid, elevates our heart rate, increases blood flow to our extremities, decreases blood flow to our internal organs and muscles, and basically gears our body up to fight something or run away from it. This hypothalamic-pituitary-adrenal axis, first described by Selye, is today known as the "fight or flight syndrome." The problem many of us have in daily life today is that most of the stressors that cause us **distress** we cannot fight or run away from, thus the lack of control or perceived lack of control. If someone cuts you off in traffic, almost causing an accident, the threat to your life will be perceived as a stressor, the reaction will likely be distress, your body will gear up to fight or flee, <u>but what can you do</u>? Sure, you can kill the person who cut you off in traffic, but that is not likely going to reduce your stress in the long-term. Conversely you can do nothing, or perhaps offer a one-finger salute and then just run away, and some people can do this and reduce the stress response. But others, faced with the same situation, are left stewing in the "juices of stress," prepared to fight or flee but unable to do anything.

And I don't use the automobile example without reason. First, the event described above is much too common today, between more heavily trafficked roads and distracted drivers eating, talking on the phone, and texting. Rare is the person who has not been cut off in traffic, so you should be able to relate to the experience. Second, if you do have a stress response and you are not able to rapidly reduce the response, your body is still geared up to fight or flee and you are, really, like an automobile with both the gas pedal and the brake pedal pushed all the way to the floorboard while the car is in drive. You do not need to be an auto mechanic to understand that if you do that to an automobile too often it won't be long before the rear-end falls out. Not that I am suggesting that your rear-end will fall out from stress. But if you cannot release either the gas pedal or the brake pedal you are stuck in a difficult position, unable to flee or fight while your body is prepared for one or the other, thus, a good analogy to our stress problems daily.

Similarly, if you are the defendant in a law suit you could certainly kill the plaintiff, just as our ancestors killed an attacking saber tooth tiger, but it is doubtful killing the plaintiff (assuming this has not already occurred and is, in fact, the cause of the litigation) will reduce your stress. You could kill the plaintiff's attorney, perhaps temporarily satisfying, but again not terribly helpful in the long-term. Or you could run away, quit practicing, leave health care, or move into a role where you no longer see patients. Some have taken this approach, going into research, becoming a medical director, or becoming a financial advisor. This type of change might help with this specific situation, but it likely offers no long-term solution. I believe there are other options available that are better.

What of this good stress, or "eustress?" If the response is the same, if the body is geared up to fight or flee, how can any stressor or stress response be characterized as "good?" Consider that I do a lot of public speaking. In multiple surveys over the years' people have related that their greatest fear is not death but fear of public speaking; death usually comes in second. Today it is fear of becoming destitute. I would place death first, personally. But as an example, I was in a speech class in college where there was a young man who had completed all the requirements for graduation from the University of Illinois with a Bachelor of Science Degree in Mechanical Engineering, save for being unable to complete, after three attempts, one required course: speech class. He made it on the fourth try!

But if you were to measure my breathing and heart rate just before I am to give a presentation, the results would look remarkably similar, if not identical, to how my body would respond to being a defendant in litigation or to any other stressor: elevated breathing, elevated heart rate, decreased blood flow to internal organs and muscles, and an increased blood flow to my skeletal muscles. My body, in short, is prepared to fight or flee. However, as I am looking <u>forward</u> to the speech, the stressor evokes this response as a way of getting me sharpened up to perform and concentrate; it is eustress that helps me be "on." A different person, faced with giving the same presentation, might perceive it differently and suffer from distress, rendering him unable to present at all and, inadvertently, confirming his fears about public speaking. If you have ever played in an athletic competition you likely experienced pre-game "jitters" or if you had to give a musical recital you were likely anxious before performing; if this helped you perform better, it would be called eustress; if the reaction caused you to perform poorly it would be considered distress.

The key point? **Same stressor, different response based on perception.** Two people perceive it as a stressor and have a stress response. But the degree of the response and the resultant outcomes are very different: one person suffers from eustress and gives a sharp, excellent presentation, while the other suffers from distress and gives a **horrible** presentation. Same stressor, two different reactions and the two different reactions are related to how the stressor is perceived. **It is not what is happening to you, it is how you respond to it that matters.**

Selye's research eventually developed a theory of physiology of stress having two components:

- A set of responses he summarized as the General Adaption Syndrome, eventually termed stress; and,

- The development of a pathological state brought about from ongoing, unrelieved stress.

Selye discovered and documented that the stress response differs from other physical responses in that stress can originate from good news or bad, from both positive and negative events. This evolved into an understanding that there is an event (**stressor**), there is our perception of the event (emotional), there is the response (**distress or eustress**), and then there is our management of the response. The challenge today, as noted, is that we often have a lack of control, or perceived lack of control, over the stressors in our life, resulting in our bodies gearing up a lot to fight or flee, life or death, when neither option is available. **And if you make everything that happens to you today a life or death proposition, you will "die" a lot.**
Stressors cause a stress response, the hypothalamic – pituitary – adrenal axis which we recognize today as the "fight or flight" syndrome left over from our prehistoric ancestors. This "fight or flight syndrome," involves a spike in body chemicals, especially adrenaline, that opens the blood vessels to your skeletal muscles, the ones that produce movement, and closes off the blood vessels to various muscles and organs not necessary to either fight or run away. Your body is flooded with sugar and fat to help you respond. Your breathing increases as does your heart rate. Cortisol is released to help process the fats into energy. Your senses heighten and you become keenly alert.

The stressor itself can be good (marriage, divorce, the birth of a child, graduation from college) or bad (the death of a loved one, divorce, job loss, or being a defendant in litigation), and often our perception of the stressor determines if it is good or bad (public speaking, but also, possibly, divorce). What is crucial is how we perceive the stressor and whether the stress response is productive or **good** (eustress), or destructive or **bad** (distress). If your response is one of distress and it continues for a long enough period the effects on your body and emotional wellbeing can be deleterious; some argue it can bring on Post-Traumatic Stress Disorder ("PTSD"), but it can also impact your life, the lives of people around you, and how you practice your profession.

According to many researchers, most of us today experience this adrenaline not in a rush but as a steady drip brought on by events both within our control (bills, work, responsibilities, "to do" lists, etc.) and outside of our control, such as the economic meltdown starting in 2007, two wars, terrorist attacks, climate change, and the like. The result of this chronic, low-level stress is our veins and arteries are constantly full of fats and sugars that spike our blood pressure and can create tiny tears in our arteries where plaque can build up, leading to cardiovascular disease and other causes of premature illness and death. Yet as noted above, the same stimulus can produce different levels of stress response; where distress uses you, you use eustress. **Control.**

3. Litigation and Health Care Professionals

First, do no harm. This oft-repeated phrase does not appear in the Hippocratic Oath, original or revised, although it does state, in the modern form, that *"Also I will, according to my ability and judgment, prescribe a regimen for the health of the sick, but I will utterly reject harm and mischief."* An equivalent phrase is found in Epidemics, Book 1 of the Hippocratic school: *"Practice two things in your dealing with disease: either help or do not harm the patient."*

Despite this exact phrase not being found anywhere in the original or modern version of the Hippocratic Oath, the basic concept is drilled into the head of every health care professional repeatedly. It was, for example, the cause of much ethical discussion within the dental profession when veneers came into existence, to be fitted in place of healthy teeth that were simply considered unattractive; among "old school" dentists harming a perfectly healthy tooth was unethical.

Regardless of the exact wording, you entered the health care profession to help people, not harm them. Yet when a malpractice claim is filed it is someone very clearly claiming they were harmed and harmed by you! And they may well have been harmed by you, but remember that does not necessarily mean that malpractice was committed.

This is the major difference, however, between you and other professionals when it comes to malpractice claims and litigation. For the most part, every profession

61

has people who have been accused of malpractice and sued for it, lawyers, accountants, insurance agents, business consultants, and investment advisers; all professionals have the potential to be sued for malpractice. Why do health care professionals in general, and doctors specifically, tend to have this over-the-top emotional reaction more so than other professions?

There are five basic reasons for this:

- Personality
- Training
- Nature of the Healing Arts
- Injury
- The Legal System

As Hans Selye is considered the "father" of modern stress research, Sara Charles, M.D., is credited with recognizing and understanding the phenomena of litigation stress in doctors. Beginning in the mid-1980s Dr. Charles, a psychiatrist who began her career at Notre Dame but did much of her pioneering work on litigation stress in physicians while at the University of Illinois in Chicago, began exploring the concept of an overly strong emotional response to malpractice claims in physicians, intrigued by her own reaction to litigation, chronicled in the book *"Defendant"* which she co-authored with her husband, Eugene Kennedy. Was her reaction unique? She was also intrigued with something that insurance companies had recognized for some time: the strongest predictor of a future malpractice claim for a physician was a previous malpractice claim. Was this coincidence or were future incidents the result of the initial claim? Did physicians practice differently after a claim? Did they view patients differently after a claim? Statistically a physician who was sued tended to have one or two more claims soon after the filing of the initial claim; was there a relationship?

Dr. Charles began conducting an extensive study, with interviews, of physicians who had been sued for malpractice and she did discover this overly strong emotional reaction, which she termed litigation stress. She also delved into why this should occur when, as noted above, all professionals, indeed all people, have the capacity to be accused of malpractice or involved in litigation and sued, but only health care providers in general, and doctors specifically, seemed to have this strong reaction.

Let me add here that as I researched this issue and met with many doctors who had been the targets of malpractice claims, **litigation stress is real**. You are not alone! In Dr. Charles' research, which has been replicated by others, she found that **95%** of all physicians involved in a malpractice suit experienced periods of severe emotional distress at various times during the litigation process, likely during periods of high activity. Some doctors have compared it to going through the five stages of grief. In discussing claims with them I have had doctors and spouses, both male and female, break down and cry, sometimes in anger, often in frustration, sometimes in fear, sometimes simply out of the natural human reaction to possibly harming someone that you never intended to harm and intended to help. My experience has taught me that much of what you will feel is based on frustration and fear: frustration because, as

Dr. Charles correctly pointed out years ago, to the physician this is about competence and a courtroom is a horrible place in which to address the competency of a health care provider, which leads to the fear that a jury will decide you as being incompetent when you really were not or are not.

But as I hope to make clear, while litigation stress is real it is an almost natural consequence for health care providers and it is not what happens to you but how you respond that matters.

PERSONALITY

All doctors tend to be highly intelligent, driven, and independent thinkers. You also frequently have a strong tendency towards self-criticism, if not before entering medical or dental school it is almost certainly learned as part of your training. This self-criticism leaves you vulnerable to feelings of guilt and doubt, and an exaggerated sense of responsibility. This can contribute to litigation stress in two ways.

First, independence can lead to isolation and dealing with litigation, based on how our legal system works, can increase isolation at a time when a support network can be crucial. Second, in terms of self-criticism it means that when things are going well, when the treatment of a patient is proceeding as expected, when a diagnosis appears to be correct, the self-criticism is still ongoing; you are still questioning, still asking if every option has been explored, if every variable has been considered and examined. Medical and dental school, and training, exacerbate this mind set.

The result is that usually by the time you are sued it is not the first shot across the bow in the saga; you are often aware that something is lurking out there, with or without a direct threat, and the filing of the malpractice claim only confirms what you already knew: either a mistake or a poor outcome occurred and you may or may not be responsible, but you feel responsible. This is the self-criticism at work. The personality of people who enter the health care profession often sets them up to feel overly emotional when there is a bad or unexpected outcome, and even more so if it seems this is confirmed by the filing of a malpractice claim.

Before moving on, a few words about loyalty. Many health care professionals are lacking in loyalty, just stating a fact, not casting aspersions, and the more educated you become (physician, dentist, or Ph.D. psychologist v. nurse, EMT, physician assistant, and the like) the more striated your loyalty tends to be. Most health care professionals are loyal to their practice and their family, and which is #1 and which is #2 often is up for grabs. God may work his/her way into the top three for some, but everybody and everything else is #3 or #4 and fading. What this means is that a lot of good people who have helped you along the way get left in the dust once they are no longer of any use to you. Some of it is personality, some of it is training. You are trained to learn from each episode, good or bad, and then move on, putting the past behind you. Some phrase it as *"I don't care what you have done for me in the past, I want to know what you are doing for me RIGHT NOW!"* I prefer to look at it as you will love me until the day you stop.

What are examples of this? Consider that the average practice administrator stays with a practice for less than five years, according to the Medical Group Management Association. In most cases that administrator has worked to get the practice into a solid position, at which point the doctors look around and ask, "Everything is going great, why do we need to pay so much money to this administrator?" So, they fire the administrator and bring in someone less expensive and less experienced...or, worse, bring in a spouse, a son, or a daughter. Things begin to deteriorate and, rapidly forgetting the past and not wanting to admit a mistake, the practice starts careening towards a cliff with decreased staff morale, increased patient dissatisfaction, more inter-office disputes, lower income, and the like. I know of one group that burned through administrators every two years and the group was in constant turmoil. They finally hired a strong administrator who showed them in crayon, then pencil, and finally in ink what was wrong and why. He fixed it. Just as health care professionals are trained to do, he found the problem and fixed it. And he stayed for 13 years!

After 13 years, he had the practice humming like a fine-tuned race car, all the divisions were in buildings the doctors owned and were making money on, all the doctors were making more money than in the past, and the practice became a lightning rod for physicians who wanted to practice **independently** and not be owned by a hospital or health care system, or worse yet by Wall Street. So, with everything in such great shape, what did one young doctor do when it was his turn to be president of the group?

You guessed it. He fired the administrator! He took it upon himself to fire the administrator, walking in at 4:00 on a Thursday afternoon and demanding keys, computers, smart phone, everything, and then escorting the administrator to the door. Only after he had completed the firing did he convene a Board meeting and tell the balance of the practice what he had done. In fact, some physicians and other employees did not hear about it until calls started coming in from local newspapers asking why the administrator was no longer there.

Note that he was not fired for cause; the group had to pay its former administrator one month of salary for every year he had been there, along with keeping all benefits in place. Where was the general counsel for the group? He inserted himself as the interim administrator and billed the practice $4,000 per week for this service, more than the administrator had been earning.

A successful conclusion? Well, before the severance pay for the fired administrator had run out the group had fallen into such disarray that it put itself up for sale. Three health care systems were initially interested, but two backed away when due diligence showed what a mess things had become. The one health system that was left standing and ended up buying the practice? It was a non-profit that needed to buy a "loser" because it was making too much money (read "*Who Killed Healthcare*" by Regina Herzlinger). Their contracts were such that several of the physicians used the opportunity to leave the practice, rendering it an even bigger money loser than it had been before. And the employees still there are now earning less money, are forced to drive miles for healthcare as they must use the new owner's health care network, and patients have started looking elsewhere for care.

And this was a practice that was over 50 years old! **Moral**: try being loyal to people who have been loyal to you, who have helped you, who have been there for you, who have done right by you. Don't discard them without a good reason as, currently, good people are increasingly hard to find. And by **building** up a core of people who have been loyal to you and you to them, you develop a **support group** if you ever find yourself facing a malpractice suit, reducing isolation!

TRAINING
The successful navigation of advanced education and training, followed in most cases by an internship, residency and perhaps a fellowship, requires self-discipline, dedication, sacrifice, and a high emotional quotient ("EQ" or the ability to delay gratification). In short, a "survival" mentality which rewards those with independent, driven, self-critical personalities who want to be or feel in control. When things go right, questioning still occurs; when something goes wrong the self-critical, doubting side takes over, regardless of poor outcome or malpractice claim. In many cases providers have emotionally beaten themselves up long before an actual claim arises.

During training the various stressors are usually in equilibrium, a balance between eustress and distress, but the suicide rate among medical students and residents still disturbs many in the health care community, as well it should. Is something being done? **Not much.** However, to add to the stressors doctors must deal with daily are the changes that have occurred in the health care system starting in the 1980s. As the health care system has evolved in the United States, physicians and dentists have found their independence working against them, with the result being that payers and health systems have assumed control of the system, taken it away from the people providing care. Remember that lack of control or a feeling of lack of control is the most common cause of distress, so the loss of control over your entire profession, the almost constant battle to garner some bit of control, increases distress and is one more stressor for you to deal with daily.

One of the most glaring examples of the changes in our health care system since the mid-1980s is the story of a successful OB/GYN who owned a home on the ocean front in Virginia. As managed care and health insurance companies ate away at his reimbursement during the 1990s he was forced to sell the family home...which was purchased by the CEO of a local health insurance company. Are you starting to feel the gas pedal and the brake pedal getting pushed down?

But beyond reimbursement are the constant decisions made "for" doctors by payers, the denial of reimbursement or refusal to pre-approve a procedure on the basis that it is not medically necessary. Or after using all your training, education and experience you feel that "X" needs to be done and the insurance company tells you that "X" is #4 on the list, and you must try #1 through #3 first. Physicians, dentists, EMTs, LCSWs, all trained to "find it and fix it" and behave in the best interest of the patient, put a great deal of effort into trying to do the right thing and the best thing for their patients, only to be thwarted by

69

insurance companies who, today, are in business to turn a profit; you can only turn a profit in health insurance by denying care. Or, if your practice is owned by a hospital or health system you may find your salary being reduced because a CFO, sitting five levels above you on the organization chart, thinks you are spending too much money on patients or not seeing enough patients. In the earliest days of commercial insurance physicians were against it as they did not want anyone sitting between them and the patient. Originally you had insurance built around professions (one of the first health insurance companies was designed to provide catastrophic coverage for teachers in Texas) or non-profit insurance companies such as Blue Cross/Blue Shield, who had to remain actuarially sound but did not reward executives with incomes well into seven and eight figures. Gradually insurance took over health care. Because of changes pushed through Congress by lobbyists, CEOs today are rewarded based on "shareholder value," how quickly they can return dividends to shareholders and how large those dividends are. To accomplish this, executives must think short-term, not long-term, and this is happening across industries, not just within health care; but with health insurance this is usually at the expense of either the patient or the person providing the service, **you**. As noted, health care can rightly be viewed as caritas or charity, while insurance is a business with its first interest being survival, its second interest being to turn a profit; how can those two disparate perspectives ever be reconciled?

Let's be honest: there was always profit in health care. But for years...for centuries... the profit went to the

people providing the care, YOU. Payment for services rendered. Today, even under the Affordable Care Act with its 20% cap on administrative costs and salaries, the profit still goes **less** to the people providing the care, the tail wagging the dog, so to speak.

Add to these stressors the highly-touted concept of outcome-based medicine, where physicians are paid based on the outcomes they produce rather than the services they provide. While theoretically this may make sense, the late Yogi Berra was once quoted as saying, *"In theory, practice and theory are the same; in practice, they are not."* As a former teacher, another profession looking at being paid based on outcomes, my response is that outcome-based reimbursement is fine, if you let me choose who comes in! Let me choose my students, let you choose your patients, and then let's have outcome-based reimbursement.

But that is not how it works. You don't get to choose only healthy, educated, compliant, adherent patients who are active partners in their care. So, in theory the idea sounds good, but in practice not so much. With each passing year doctors have found their independence (and the Taft-Hartley Act) has kept them from organizing to defend their profession, defend their turf, while the health insurance companies, Big Pharma, and the hospitals, with well-heeled lobbyists and the ability to speak with one voice, have assumed control of the health care system. You spend years studying and learning about your profession, and usually incur a great deal of debt doing so, work to develop a profession that is never pure science, never pure statistics but is largely still art, only to enter a profession where you are not only told what you can and

71

cannot do but whether you will be paid for it and how much!   Or as one lobbyist for the health insurance companies stated (my wife won't let me name him as I already have had two confrontations with him), "*It is the duty of the health insurance industry to ensure physicians and patients don't steal health care.*" Say what?

This current system means a lack of control for you and a lack of control, or perceived lack of control, contributes to stress, so many health care providers are dealing with ongoing, low-level distress daily. Enhanced scientific studies are showing that constant low-level distress can trigger a cascading flow of chemicals that have a long-term deleterious effect on the body, the exact impact that Hans Selye, with less science and more art to work from, reported on over 70 years ago. One result of this unremitting distress is a reported increase in burnout among health care providers, even before they incur a malpractice claim.   Articles on physician burnout are showing up with increasing regularity. But "worn out" may be more accurate.

THE NATURE OF THE HEALING ARTS

If you were not fiercely independent before school and training, you likely were by the time you finished. Success in medical or dental school is often predicated on guilt ("Have I done enough?") and competition.   This is crucial to successful completion of your education and training, and crucial to building a successful practice, in that it is usually you and the patient, one-on-one, and it is intensely personal.   But it also can leave you intensely isolated. This goes to the identity you develop as a health care professional, but it is too easy to get confused between "**who you are**" and "**what you do**." You are a human being, beautiful but imperfect. That is who you are. You are a practitioner of the healing arts: that is WHAT you do, not who you are.

But you can, too easily, meld these together. It is evidenced in the workaholism so rampant in the healing arts, but it is also why there is so much burnout and why there is such a tendency towards litigation stress. The malpractice claim is about what you did based on what you do, but you likely will internalize it as a claim against **WHO** you are. This is an intensely personal and isolating aspect of the healing arts that makes you more prone to a severe over-reaction to litigation. Therefore, as I researched litigation stress, it became my opinion that a lack of litigation stress in a health care provider may be more of a concern than litigation stress itself.

In addition, the nature of practicing the healing arts is often packed with emotion; often you are asked to deal with people during their most vulnerable, important, or stressful times in their lives and this cannot help but impact you. I have sometimes found myself comparing what you do to an episode of an old TV series, "The Twilight Zone." In one episode, the main character was a "sin eater." Essentially it was a swindle to get free food: people would bring food to the "sin eater" and as he ate the food he "ate away" their sins. Except in this episode (spoiler alert if you have not seen it and plan to rent it) as the sin eater eats the food he is actually consuming the sins of the person who brought him the food and the sins are many, causing the sin eater to gradually lose his mind.

Sort of sounds like the practice of health care? You must not only deal with your own emotions, in what is

73

often an emotion-packed atmosphere, but also the emotions of the patient and, perhaps, the patient's spouse and/or family. Put even more simply, I hate to lose, therefore I would likely not last very long in health care as, despite your best efforts, sometimes you lose. Every loss would stay with me much too long and I am writing this with the hope that something I say in here reaches you and keeps you from getting eaten up. Because in your dreams, when you were thinking about being a physician or dentist or other health care provider, you always won, right? You always saved the day! That, as you have discovered, is not reality.

Trying to be perfect in every way, every day, will eat up anyone. You must be a good person, good diagnostician, a good business person, and always with the legal system hanging over your shoulder. I want to help control that.

When confronted with a malpractice claim, studies and anecdotal reports have found that health care providers reported feelings of:

- **Isolation**
- **Negative self-worth**
- **Negative self-image**
- **Severe emotional response**
- **Emotional volatility**
- **Insecurity**
- **Anxiety**
- **Suicide ideation**

How severe the reaction is depends in part on the person (**how well did you handle stress before the claim?**) and the circumstances (were you negligent or do you feel as if you were negligent?) Based on education, training and personality, the probability is strong that you will believe you were negligent even if you were not, and it will take some time and convincing from third parties to convince you that you were not negligent, if that is the case.

These feelings often expressed themselves as:

- **Depression**
- **Frustration**
- **Irritability**
- **Insomnia**
- **Anger**
- **Fatigue**
- **Eating disorders**
- **Alcohol or other drug use**
- **Family and/or marital problems**
- **Health complications**

In addition to the potential impacts listed above happening to you individually, there is your organization to consider. When a member of a health care practice is involved in a malpractice claim, organizations report being impacted by:

- **An increase in accidents**
- **Reduced productivity**

- **Increased errors**
- **Increased absenteeism**
- **Unpreparedness**
- **Increased use of sick leave**
- **Premature retirement**
- **Increased job dissatisfaction**
- **Impaired decision-making**

All of the above is exacerbated by the legal process as you will be instructed to not talk about the case except under the direction of your attorney, to protect attorney-client privilege. You will WANT to talk about the case, confirm that you did nothing wrong, and you will get that chance, but do so at the direction of your attorney because you will be asked who you have discussed the case with and anyone you did discuss the case with will be deposed; if they are critical of your care in any way they could end up as a witness against you.

But remember that all of the above is a result of the claim against you, not the specifics of the claim. Therefore, establishing a relationship with a primary care physician, if you don't have one already, is very important. But you will also likely benefit from establishing a relationship with a mental health professional, be it a Licensed Clinical Social Worker, psychologist, psychiatrist, or the like. Not only can you talk freely about the emotions, feelings, and thoughts you have been dealing with because of the claim, these conversations are covered by privilege and cannot be disclosed.

What is the most important take-away from the above? **You are not alone**. You are not the only one who is reacting this way or has reacted this _, เง a malpractice claim. You are not only not alone, your feelings and thoughts are normal and the result of litigation stress,

INJURY

Perhaps that which sets you up for litigation stress more than any other profession is physical injury. If any other profession commits an alleged act of malpractice, usually no one suffers a **physical** injury. Attorneys, accountants, insurance agents and the like may commit an alleged act of malpractice, but it they do so they are usually not forced to deal with a physically injured party. And, as noted, since you are often aware of the injury or bad outcome, the arrival of a malpractice claim is like the exclamation point at the end of a sentence: "*I know there was a bad outcome, I don't need a malpractice claim to remind me!*" The self-criticism and doubt were there all along.

Yet a bad outcome or injury does not automatically mean that malpractice was committed. In fact, the outcome that was accomplished might have been the best outcome that anyone short of a miracle worker could have accomplished, yet a malpractice claim is filed. Why? Because it is usually the only way a person can be heard and seek redress under our current civil legal system. The only exception to this rule: our worker compensation system which, on a state-by-state basis, allows for an injured employee to be made whole, or as close to whole as possible, without resorting to the civil legal system (although attempts are being made to change this).

77

There is an expression in service-oriented industries about "under-promising and over-delivering." In health care, we call it getting a patient's expectations in line with the likely outcome, a part of the informed consent process. In the case of the surgeon noted previously, who was taking on cases other surgeons were refusing, as well intentioned as he was he essentially was over-promising and then, in the eyes of the patient (and the plaintiff's attorney), under-delivering. That is a recipe for a malpractice claim and the only way, in most cases, to resolve this is through litigation.

The challenge is that we have a massively imperfect civil legal system that is too expensive, too time consuming, much too adversarial, and fed by insurance money. Yet when people talk about "tort reform" what they usually mean is making it more difficult for an injured party to seek redress.

Malcolm Gladwell discusses this in his book "*David and Goliath*" where he refers to the "***Principle of Legitimacy***" and the fact that it is based on three things:

1. **People who are asked to obey authority must feel as if they have a voice, that if they speak up they will be heard.**
2. **The law at issue must be predictable, there must be reasonable expectation that the rules today are going to roughly be the same tomorrow.**
3. **The authority must be fair; it cannot treat one group differently from another.**

Gladwell, Malcom, "*David and Goliath*", p 154

78

Many people, perhaps most, somehow understand this instinctively, be they parents, teachers, or the military. When I first entered the teaching profession I had an old assistant principal pull me aside and tell me "*Do not make a rule unless you intend to enforce it 100% of the time or it will cause you headaches.*" I learned that he was correct, although I learned the hard way. He also told me not to smile in class until Thanksgiving! Get expectations in line!

Not making a rule unless you intend to enforce it 100% of the time adheres to the "Principle of Legitimacy," but is close to 180 degrees the opposite of our civil legal system today. We have seen and heard of too many examples of the law being applied in a non-uniform manner, civil and criminal, and this includes malpractice cases where we have heard of a jury that should have awarded damages and did not, as well as fewer times when a jury should NOT have awarded damages and did. Finally, as someone forgotten by me once stated, "*The rich are different, they've got money.*" It might have been Oscar Wilde. A staunch tort reform U.S. Representative from a Northeastern state continued to rail on about the abuses of the legal system undermining doctors and needlessly increasing the cost of health care, while he was quietly settling, acting as his own attorney, a $900,000 malpractice claim in the name of his wife. Would a construction worker whose wife suffered the same injury be afforded the same treatment? I would argue not.

All of this shows how the civil legal system does not work in a uniform manner; however, it also supports multiple studies, using closed medical record reviews, that show many more cases of medical negligence occur than there are claims filed, including two Harvard studies, one released in 1991 (*Relation between Malpractice Claims and Adverse Events Due to Negligence — Results of the Harvard Medical Practice Study III* - A. Russell Localio, J.D., M.P.H., M.S., Ann G. Lawthers, Sc.D., Troyen A. Brennan, M.D., J.D., M.P.H., Nan M. Laird, Ph.D., Liesi E. Hebert, Sc.D., Lynn M. Peterson, M.D., Joseph P. Newhouse, Ph.D., Paul C. Weiler, LL.M., and Howard H. Hiatt, M.D. N Engl J Med 1991; 325:245-251July 25, 1991 DOI: 10.1056/NEJM199107253250405) and another conducted after the hard insurance market in 2006 by researchers from the Harvard School of Public Health (HSPH) and Brigham and Women's Hospital (the findings appeared in the May 11, 2006 issue of The New England Journal of Medicine.

The researchers analyzed past malpractice claims and closed medical records to judge the volume of "meritless" lawsuits and determine their outcomes. Their findings suggested that portraits of a malpractice system riddled with frivolous lawsuits are overblown. Although nearly one third of claims lacked clear-cut evidence of medical error, most of these suits did not receive compensation. In fact, the number of meritorious claims that did not get paid was larger than the group of meritless claims that were paid (emphasis added).

To summarize the results of these studies for the relevance of this publication, in which malpractice claims were matched to inpatient medical records, demonstrate that the civil justice system only infrequently compensates injured patients, and rarely identifies and holds health care providers accountable for substandard medical care. Although malpractice litigation may fulfill its social objectives, support for its preservation persists in part because of *the perception* that other methods of ensuring a high quality of care and redressing patients' grievances have proved to be inadequate. The abandonment of malpractice litigation is unlikely unless credible systems and procedures, supported by the public, are instituted to guarantee professional accountability to patients.

Further, most malpractice claims that did not involve error did NOT receive compensation and if they did the compensation was lower than payments made for claims that did involve error. Claims that did not involve error absorbed a relatively small portion of the overall costs. The key findings in both studies were that more patients were injured than there were claims filed, and of the claims filed the civil system "got it right" about 75% of the time. The malpractice system, according to these and other studies, is not inundated with groundless claims that contribute to a "lottery mentality" that drive up the cost of health care.

In a separate study released May 10, 2006 by the Robert Wood Johnson Foundation's Synthesis Project, the effects of the recent increases in malpractice insurance premiums on the delivery of health care services and the impacts of state tort reforms were examined. Reviewing existing studies, the report concluded that the deteriorating liability environment has had only a modest effect on the supply of physician services. Aside from caps on noneconomic damages, most tort reforms adopted by states in response to malpractice crises have not been effective in boosting physician supply or reducing insurance or litigation costs. Damages caps help constrain

81

growth in litigation costs and insurance premiums over time, but disproportionately burden the most severely injured patients (the very young, the very old, the poor, and stay-at-home parents, those with little in the way of economic damages).

The take away is to not get caught up in the belief that the tort system is unfair to health care professionals, but to understand that the tort system is uniformly not uniform. The problem is not malpractice, it is litigation. In our current tort system competency of health care providers is erroneously tied to compensation; patients must allege negligence because they don't get any money otherwise. But the courtroom is an improper forum to address competency. As the studies above, and other studies illustrate, society and physicians need to find a way to separate the two notions of competency and litigation, that a trial is genuinely not a search for the truth (unless you end up on "*Judge Judy*").

"It would be helpful if doctors could learn to separate the alleged act of malpractice from the malpractice claim; one is an issue of medical competence, the other is a business/legal transaction, an exchange of money in return for alleged negligence." -Sara C. Charles, M.D.

What Dr. Charles notes above is how most professionals can handle a claim of negligence, as a nuisance, as part of doing business. There may well be anger because a professional reputation has suffered an insult, but other professionals, when charged with professional negligence, are more likely to walk through the front door of the family home after work, take off his suit and tie, and in doing so "take off" the malpractice claim until returning to work the next day. The training and personality of doctors, along with the nature of health care, leaves "what you do" tied tightly with "who you are" and "what you do" is be a doctor or other health care provider 24 x 7 x 365.

Finally, while you were likely dealing with the maelstrom of all these ongoing stressors you must focus on daily, I would be remiss if I did not point out one thing: during the hard insurance market from 2000-2006, when malpractice insurance premiums seemingly doubled every year, 29 states passed medical malpractice tort reform. **The impact of this tort reform on the cost of health care? None. Zero. No impact.** Health insurance premiums and costs increased at the same rate in the tort reform states as in those states that did not pass tort reform. In the state where I live, Virginia, we have medical malpractice laws that health care providers in most other states would love to have: a hard cap per claim (not per defendant), with a neurologic birth injury fund. We mandate a certificate by an expert before a case can go forward. In other words, Virginia is likely the highest risk/lowest reward state in the country for plaintiff's attorneys when it comes to filing a malpractice claim. Is this reflected in the cost of malpractice insurance? Yes, it is relatively low in Virginia even though the average indemnity payment in Virginia in 2015, per the National Practitioner Data Bank, was approximately $100,000 higher than the national average (it was $100,000 lower than the national average in 1990) and Virginia physicians are forced by the hospitals to carry limits equal to or greater than the malpractice cap (currently $2.3 million per claim 07/01/2017, on its way to $3 million per claim in 2031). Is it reflected in the cost of health care and health insurance premiums? No.

So, if you are involved in a malpractice claim, you who has been trained to find it and fix it, but first do no harm, you are looking at a former patient you may have harmed, or at least has been harmed, and you are now being sued for it. This is one big thing that separates a medical malpractice claim from other malpractice claims, the physical injury.

Which brings me to…

THE LEGAL SYSTEM

It is often said that we are a nation of laws and it is true, but it is because we are not a nation of honor. If the global economic meltdown that began in 2007 and resulted in the Great Recession had been caused by Japanese firms, not only would leaders have resigned due to dishonor and shame, some of them may have committed Harakiri! In the U.S., perpetrators were rewarded with vast, obscene, incomprehensible amounts of money. While millions lost their jobs, incomes, health insurance, homes, retirement incomes and more, the people who caused this were rewarded and rewarded handsomely. PTSD for the masses?

The point being, a huge source of your distress will be with the civil legal system. The challenge is this: the legal system is all about the legal system, especially civil law as opposed to criminal law. It is not about right and wrong or good and bad…**unless and until it gets in front of a jury** (which ironically may be your personal worst nightmare). The legal profession is about the practice of the legal profession, but that swings from attorneys trying to make the world a better place to attorneys who became attorneys to find ways to break the law and not get caught, or bend the law or play with it. And **if you find an attorney who wants to make the world a better place, he/she will have to get just as down and dirty as the opposition**. There was a time when lawyers took their positions as <u>officers of the court</u> seriously; today the ethics concerning this still exist in state and national Bar Association guidelines, but usually exist in name only when it comes to punishing lawyers for misconduct. If you find yourself reading certain sections of this book and thinking to yourself that there must be a better way to resolve disputes, you are correct!

Fortunately, this "Rambo-lawyering," as it is sometimes called, is not 100% accurate with a malpractice claim, which is heavily fact driven. The very essence of the concept of negligence is that an accident occurred that should not have, but I have rarely heard or read about anyone accusing a doctor of intentionally injuring a patient.

Are changes needed in our civil legal system? Yes. Does all that preceded this section speak for changes in the civil legal system? Yes, but let me clarify a few things. **First**, in America today the tort system is usually the only way for an injured person to be made whole, or as whole as possible. In litigation one person must lose and one person must win, period. This is expensive, time consuming, adversarial, usually nasty, emotionally draining for both the plaintiff (patient) and defendant or defendants, and uniformly NOT uniform.

Let me give you an example of what I mean by that last statement. I managed a claim once where a 67-year-old woman was having a laser procedure done to remove wrinkles (insert your own comment about someone getting wrinkles removed at 67, my age as I write this and I have wrinkles; e-mail me and I'll send you a picture). Somehow, she received burns on her face and I say "somehow" because there was no evidence, based on the record, that anything was performed improperly, so short of a machine malfunction (which would not have been the fault of the physician or the aesthetician) it was going to be a difficult case for the plaintiff's attorney to prove. Unfortunately, in this case the physician demanded the case NOT be settled as she insisted that she did nothing wrong…until the Friday before a Monday trial when she suddenly demanded the case be settled at any cost as she did not want to go to trial. Except it doesn't work that way.

The case was not settled over the weekend, the plaintiff's attorney and the defense attorneys had told me the physician was going to do very poorly on the stand (despite all the preparation work with her by the defense) and she did not disappoint, even calling the plaintiff's attorney by his first name, a dumb move. The jury did not like her, did not find her believable, and rendered a verdict against her in excess of $650,000.

Now we move about 90 miles down the road to a different jurisdiction, same plaintiff's attorney, same laser machine, same injury to a woman in her **30s**, different physician. Jury verdict? $125,000. The difference? A likeable physician, no evidence of fault, but the jury felt the patient needed to be compensated.   Thus, the lack of uniformity in the system.

I don't know if I came up with this statement or read it somewhere, but I have found **time** to be a friend of the truth and an enemy of a lie. So as a fitting ending to the two related claims above, it turns out the device was defective. It was a defectively designed laser that was causing the problems, not the medical practitioners, and the device was eventually taken off the market.   One expert witness referred to it as a "blow torch." Thus, the same plaintiff's attorney who tried both cases also had a products liability case filed in a third jurisdiction on the chance the juries blamed the machines and not the physicians. Uniformly not a uniform system. But while I just told you a couple of stories that might have scared the bejeezus out of you, remember that doctors win at trial about 80% of the time, regardless of the insurance company involved.

Second, I am not anti-plaintiff's attorney, as so many in the insurance and health care industries are. There was even a widely-reported story some years ago of a plaintiff's attorney with a pregnant wife who moved to a South Carolina town that only had one OB/GYN group...which refused to treat the pregnant woman because her husband was a plaintiff's attorney. She had to drive to another town for treatment.

Plaintiff's attorneys are not the reason for escalating tort costs or escalating health care costs or escalating malpractice claims; just as student loans are often blamed for increases in college tuition ("the money is there, let's get our cut of it"), the use of deep pockets and, often, insurance money results in corporate defense attorneys dragging cases out for years that could be settled in days or weeks, months at worst, corporate or medical. In medical malpractice claims, as noted, there is a measure called the "occurrence-to-settlement lag," the time it takes between when an injury occurs and when a claim closes. Nationally the average occurrence-to-settlement lag for several years has been around 4.9 years. During this time the injured patient, if due compensation, is not being compensated, the legal costs of the claim are escalating, and the distress for the doctor is ongoing. As noted, plaintiff's attorneys basically work on a wing and a prayer; they do not take a case unless they think they can get it to a jury, which means navigating all the various laws and precedent setting cases in each state and the obstacles set up by the defense attorneys. It often takes six-to-nine months just to get a court to say it's OK for a case to go forward, to get started.

As a plaintiff attorney will only take a case if he/she believes it can get to a jury trial, it is the job of defense attorneys to prevent a case from getting to trial. Therefore, many filed civil suits never get to trial (read "*The Myth of Moral Justice*" by Thane Rosenbaum, one of the books recommended at the end of this for additional reading). Once a case gets to a jury the law is usually already settled and the jury is simply asked to assess right and wrong, which juries do amazingly well. This is one reason doctors usually win about 80% of jury trials; it is not because of frivolous lawsuits or overzealous plaintiff's attorneys, but because a jury, when only presented with facts and not legal mumbo jumbo, can usually determine right from wrong and good from bad. Not always, but usually.

Viewed another way, I have mentioned that essentially all medical professional liability insurance companies claim they win 80% or more of the cases they take to trial. Most of these insurance companies use the same defense attorneys. Thus, is that 80% success rate because of the insurance company, the defense attorneys, **or** the fact that the juries, when presented with the facts and nothing but the facts, usually make the right call about whether an actual act of negligence occurred?

Third, on the other side from the plaintiff's attorney, who only gets a fee if he/she wins a settlement or verdict, is the defense attorney. You have malpractice insurance so the insurance company can pay an attorney to defend you. Medical malpractice defense practice is different from corporate defense practice. In corporate defense, unless you have two equally-sized corporations going after each other, you have a plaintiff's attorney on one side who is likely representing a client who was legitimately harmed by a corporation that is protected by deep pockets, insurance money or both, and the defendant feels it is too big and important to be touched, so it has done something most people would consider to be indefensible. The plaintiff's attorney must assess if the case can survive all the legal roadblocks, either in state law, federal law or by precedent that will be thrown up by these corporate attorneys defending the indefensible, how long it will take, how expensive it will be, all in the hope the case can get to a jury. If the case can get to a jury, the jury will very easily be able to tell right from wrong, good from bad, and render a just verdict. Not every time, but most of the time. Therefore, the job of a **corporate** defense attorney, in defending the indefensible, is to

.

delay, obfuscate, run up costs for the plaintiff's attorney and the plaintiff, seek repeated continuances, all to beat the plaintiff down so that eventually a steeply one-sided settlement is proffered and, hopefully, accepted by the plaintiff out of exhaustion, and the defense attorney's client never sees the inside of a courtroom. And the settlement is to be kept confidential, so the public and, in some cases, authorities never learn of the wrongdoing. I want to leave religion and politics out of this as much as possible, but this is how Donald Trump has bragged he handles all litigation against him: wear the other side down and settle for pennies on the dollar, then declare a landslide victory. If he did not brag about doing it, I would not have mentioned it. As the president of a company I worked for phrased it, the goal is for the side with money to *make the juice not worth the squeeze*." As one of my attorneys put it, it is like being dragged nekkid through a briar patch. Slowly.

Of course, this same corporate president had a basic philosophy towards life that was summed up as, "It doesn't matter if you win or lose, as long as you kill the other person."

The good news? **This is not how a medical malpractice case usually works**. It is still adversarial and the attorneys involved can make it more so. Sometimes a deposition can get rough, for both you and the plaintiff. More frustrating to you is that you would like the case to be a scientific inquiry and it often ends up, if it goes on long enough, as theatre instead. Alternative Dispute Resolution can reduce the nastiness once the process gets to a mediation or arbitration because the doctor and patient start out sitting in the same room, which allows them to be human beings if only for a few minutes.

A medical malpractice case usually centers around the **standard of care** and if it was followed: as you worked your way towards a differential diagnosis did you follow standard reasoning (if you hear hoofbeats think horses not zebras) and was the treatment appropriate based on the diagnosis. Is there a lot of wiggle room there? Yes. Get two doctors arguing about this you get three opinions. But this is what most malpractice cases center around: given all available information did you do what a reasonable and prudent (not heroic) health care professional would have done?

Standard of Care
What a reasonable person who is comparably trained would do or not do under the same or similar circumstances. You don't have to always be right, you just must act reasonably, given the circumstances.

There was a time when the standard of care was different from state to state and within different jurisdictions of a state (think rural v. urban). Today most courts accept that there is, at the least, agreement on a statewide basis, which is often a disservice to doctors working in underserved, rural areas.

In addition, this is one of the concerns with outcome based medicine; if you, with good reason, deviate from the protocol as established by an Accountable Care Organization, commercial payer, some think tank, or the government and have a bad outcome, is it de facto malpractice? What if there was a good reason to deviate, a reason based on logic and science and experience? Or, what if you follow the protocol the payer insists on, even if you disagree with it, and there is a bad outcome; is it de facto malpractice? If you are forced to refer to a specialist inside an Accountable Care Organization when you know a different specialist would be better for a specific procedure and there is a bad outcome, who is at fault? Once upon a time the standard of care was local; urban doctors were held to slightly different standards than rural doctors. But even then, the standard of care is not set in stone; as your claim proceeds through what is called discovery both your attorney and the plaintiff's attorney will find experts to support their respective positions (and in many states tort reform now mandates some sort of certification from a doctor that there is a reasonable expectation the plaintiff does have grounds on which to base the claim). More on discovery in the next chapter, but it is one of two crucial points before trial.

Remember that a malpractice claim is a civil suit, not criminal. Unless you have broken some laws, no one is going to prison. **If you have children and they are made aware of the suit or claim, make sure they know this so their imaginations do not run wild!**

Also, remember that a malpractice claim is a negligence claim; in a civil proceeding the burden of proof is on the plaintiff to prove negligence was committed, not beyond a shadow of a doubt but based on a preponderance of the evidence. Legally this means that all four of the following usually must be proven for a case of negligence to be made (although they often are not):

.

1. Doctor-Patient Relationship. This is usually not at issue but weird circumstances have created a duty in the past and could in the future. When does your duty begin? In most states, it begins when a patient schedules an appointment; courts have ruled that this does not necessarily mean that a relationship has been formed, but when the patient asks to be seen, your staff asks why, the patient gives a reason and an appointment is made, courts have ruled that a duty to treat has been established. But other relationships have been formed in a less casual manner. When managed care was first booming during the 1980s and 1990s (and remember that Accountable Care Organizations are basically managed care on steroids), a doctor would sign up to participate and be assigned a list of patients who had contracted with the managed care organization ("MCO"). The name of the doctor would be sent to the patient with the patient being given the option of changing if so desired, but many did not. What would then sometimes happen is the patient would have to go to the emergency room, when asked for the name of the primary care physician would give the name of the one assigned by the MCO, he/she would be called and not recognize the name of the patient as the patient had never been seen in the office, and the physician would direct the ER to contact the on-call physician. Did the physician who was assigned the patient by the MCO have a physician-patient relationship, a duty to treat? Multiple courts, based on the wording of

93

.

MCO contracts, answered "yes!" So, you could have a duty to treat a patient that you have never seen. When this relationship forms is also of concern for those specialties that do not routinely see patients, such as radiologists and pathologists; seeing the patient's films or slides and then communicating with the treating physician will most assuredly constitute the formation of a relationship. Similarly, with general dentists who refer to periodontists, endodontists, or the like: each dentist has a relationship with that patient.

2. Breach of the duty to treat. More commonly this is called a "breach of the standard of care" and it is what most malpractice cases hinge upon. It will be alleged that you did something you should not have done; or, it will be alleged that you did NOT do something that you should have done. In either case, it will be alleged that your actions fell below the acceptable standard of care, usually something that is not set in stone. The plaintiff will try to (or in many states today must) find at least one expert to say you breached the standard of care, while the attorney retained for you by your insurance company will try to find experts that are supportive of the care you rendered. If both sides can develop strong expert opinions the case will often go to a jury trial or mediation; if one side can develop strong experts and the other side cannot, the case will quickly tilt one way or the other depending on who is having trouble finding experts. If the plaintiff cannot find solid expert

witnesses the case should eventually go away; if the defense (your side) cannot find solid experts the case may quickly become a settlement candidate. And keep in mind that there are expert witnesses and fact witnesses, and expert witnesses will speak to both standard of care and to proximate cause.

3. Harm or injury. Historically this meant a physical injury that resulted in economic damages, but the tort system changed during the 1970s in part due to court decisions recognizing non-economic and non-physical injuries as being worthy of compensation. These non-economic injuries are frequently called "pain and suffering" injuries and were the centerpiece of much of the tort reform passed during the hard insurance market from 2002-2006. Caps were placed on non-economic damages, usually $250,000, which made it difficult (meaning non-profitable) for a plaintiff's attorney to take a case with limited economic damages; historically plaintiff attorneys will state that a malpractice case must be worth at least $250,000 for it to be worth the risk of taking it. Too much risk, not enough reward. A uniformly non-uniform civil legal system. As you likely have already figured out, a cap on non-economic damages makes it difficult to file a malpractice claim on behalf of the very young, the very old, or stay-at-home parents, those who do not have economic damages (primarily lost present and future wages). At last count seven of the 29 states that passed caps on non-economic damages had the

laws overturned as being a violation of the state constitution. As previously noted, what was interesting to a lot of observers was the impact on the cost of health care in the states where these caps were passed: $0. The cost of health care in states where caps were passed increased the same as in states without caps. This seems to negate the argument that tort reform will reverse the trend of increasing health care costs due to defensive medicine. In addition, in states with non-economic damage caps the plaintiff's attorneys have found one way around this issue is to bring in economic experts who can develop and explain the estimated cost of a "life care plan" for an injured person with limited economic damages.

Perhaps the "poster child" for an argument against these caps was a 25-year-old woman in Texas. Texas passed a $250,000 cap on non-economic damages during the hard insurance market. This young lady worked as a nail technician. She was having problems with her leg and visited the local emergency room three times, where it was missed that she had a blood clot. Eventually she lost her leg in a below-the-knee amputation. Despite clear negligence and a missed diagnosis, no plaintiff's firm in Dallas would take the case. Why? As a nail technician, she could perform her job sitting down, so it could be argued she had no economic loss, only emotional or "soft" damages. As might be expected, this does not generate good publicity for these caps.

4. Proximate Cause. Proximate cause refers to the concept that there was a direct relationship between any alleged breach of the standard of care and the injury. This may sound cut-and-dried but it sometimes is not. For example, it has often been discussed in insurance underwriting circles how it is possible for an oncologist to ever be sued for malpractice: you have one of two outcomes, life or death, and death is what will happen if you do nothing, so if you do something and death still occurs, as it so often does despite all the incredible breakthroughs in recent years, how can there be any relationship between the care that was rendered and the outcome? Even if the doctor did something wrong but it did not change the treatment or prognosis, there should be no finding of negligence as the injury is unrelated to the breach of the standard of care, there is no proximate cause. This is common in failure to diagnose or late diagnosis of cancer, where there was a miss or a delay, but that error did not result in any change to the treatment plan or prognosis, or even to the outcome. In black and white this seems simple, but in reality it is not as you are essentially telling a jury that the doctor did something wrong, but no money should be given to the patient (or the patient's estate). In addition, different states have different laws on contributory negligence. Contributory negligence refers to actions taken by the patient, coincidental with care, which contributed to the bad outcome; actions undertaken by the patient before

treatment do not count, right or wrong. During my time handling claims we tried two claims based on contributory negligence and lost both. The biggest reason? Lack of documentation as to the patient's behavior, especially missing phone call information.

So, to prove negligence a plaintiff is supposed to convince, first, a judge and then, if you get far enough, a jury that all four elements of the theory of negligence were met: that a duty was owed, the duty was breached, there was harm or injury, and there was a relationship between the breach of duty and the injury. Absent any one of these four components it can be argued that negligence did not occur.

THE CLAIM PROCESS

One of the most important activities you should undertake is educating yourself on the claim process in your state or jurisdiction. Remember that most of the distress we experience today is due to a lack of control or perceived lack of control, something that tends to make health care professionals more uncomfortable than the average person; educating yourself on the process you will be going through, whether you ever actually get to trial or not, will not give you actual control over the process, but the knowledge will help reduce your distress because you will know what to expect. In addition, it will decrease or eliminate surprises during the process. You can research this information yourself, ask your assigned attorney or insurance company claims adjuster for this information, or access it on line.

In most states, the claim process will follow a similar path and one other thing you can do, in addition to educating yourself on the process, is to get with the attorney assigned to you by the insurance company as soon as possible and become familiar with this team that will be defending you, learn how he/she will work, get the likely timing of events, and ask for when your involvement will be necessary. It is important to note that while I mentioned the occurrence-to-settlement lag time is usually between four and five years, it does not mean that you will be physically involved, or tied up time-wise, for that entire time; there will be bursts of activity followed by weeks or months of little or nothing going on that requires your involvement. This can make the process more stressful for some as, again, it is out of your control, but being aware of it helps you deal with it. By knowing as much as possible about the process and what to expect gives you some feeling of control over the situation and can help reduce the stress response; knowledge is power in this case.

Normally the process starts with some sort of notice from an attorney that either a claim or suit is going to be filed or it may be an actual notice that a claim or law suit has been filed. Some key points about this:

- You will likely be served notice by a legal process server or perhaps a sheriff, depending on the jurisdiction and the plaintiff's attorney.
- Whatever document you are served with carries some time requirements for you to respond, so make sure that all staff members are instructed to either refuse service until you are there to sign for

.

it (which may or may not delay service) or know that it needs to get into your hands or the practice manager's hands immediately, so that it can get to the insurance company as quickly as possible. I prefer that my customers contact me and I then relay the information to the insurance company. Regardless of who you contact, failure to respond in a timely fashion can cause the claim to go into default, essentially meaning that you have admitted all allegations are true; if this happens the insurance company can walk away from covering the claim as failing to promptly respond has jeopardized its chance to defend the claim.

- Once you have received it, as noted, a clock is ticking, in most states even if it is just a request for medical records; therefore, you immediately want to contact either your insurance agent or insurance company, notify them of what you have received, and follow their instructions. A note about notifying your insurance agent: not all insurance companies do an equal job of letting insurance agents know about claims and so we are frequently surprised when, a couple of months before renewal, we learn that a doctor or practice has had two or three claims in the last year. So, agents like to be notified and will then accept the responsibility of notifying the insurance company if you have not already done so. However, you can certainly contact the insurance company directly.

- Do not immediately contact an attorney. The insurance company will likely give you some input into the selection of defense attorney, but depending on the specifics of the claim you may want to use attorney Jones but the company knows that attorney Smith has an outstanding record of accomplishment and a lot of experience and expertise with claims such as your claim, and would prefer attorney Smith handle the claim. Unless the chemistry between you and attorney Smith is horrendous it is recommended you go with the insurance company's recommended attorney, but make sure the company gives you the reason. If the reason is attorney Smith is $100 per hour less expensive than attorney Jones, don't be afraid to fight for the attorney you want to use.

- Finally, once you receive notice of a claim or potential claim do not discuss the facts of the case with anyone until you are under the protection of an attorney. Once an attorney has been assigned to you and you have a chance to meet with him/her to discuss the case you will be given further directions on who you can talk to and about what, as acting at the direction of your attorney affords you the protection of attorney-client privilege. However, this privilege can be breached by certain actions or conversations and this is where it can be challenging for a doctor: at a time when you really want to talk about the case, when you want to seek confirmation of your care, when you want to act as a human being and confirm you did nothing wrong, you must maintain silence about the facts of the case. You can discuss that a case exists and you can, at your discretion, discuss your feelings, your anger, your frustration, your fear, just not the facts. The reason for this is for your own protection. You will be asked at some point in discovery who you have discussed the case with and anyone you name will then be deposed; if, under oath, they disagree with or question any aspect of your care they could end up as a witness against you. Despite you wanting to talk about the case A LOT, resist the urge and follow the directions of your attorney.

Once the claim or suit papers are in the hands of the attorney assigned by the insurance company to defend you (I stated it that way because, while it may seem weird, the attorney is representing you, not the insurance company...admittedly sometimes a difficult line to walk) the attorney will file some sort of motion to dismiss the claim, usually called a **demurrer**. This is done especially if facts are lacking in the suit papers that make it difficult for the defense attorney to know what the case is about or evidence supporting the allegations is weak. The court can find in favor of the plaintiff, deny the demurrer, and schedule a hearing to set a trial date and a pre-trial scheduling order; or, the court can find in favor of the defense, grant the demurrer, and give the plaintiff time to "cure" the pleading or claim, to correct any weaknesses or vagueness in the filing, allow the plaintiff to re-file the suit, and then go through the process again. Normally if the plaintiff's attorney has done the proper amount of homework the claim or suit papers will be drawn up in such a way that the court will allow the case to proceed.

Once the case can proceed, **discovery** begins. In simple terms, discovery is supposed to be a process whereby each side learns or tries to learn what the other side knows or what information or knowledge it has. During this early stage expert witnesses will be sought out by both sides. As noted, in many states today tort reform has been passed that mandates a plaintiff have an affidavit from an expert stating that the claim has merit, based on his/her opinion. The strength of these laws varies from state-to-state; in some states, it must be a doctor or other professional specifically practicing your specialty, in other states it can come from any doctor or affiliated professional.

Each side will look for the strongest experts and strongest opinions it can find to support its position. One of the most difficult situations for a doctor is the inability of the defense to find any solid experts to defend the care that was rendered; if the defense cannot find any experts to defend the care that was rendered it most certainly should consider settlement of the case. This does not happen often, but it does happen and two notes of caution related to this: document, document, document; and, don't let the patient drive the treatment plan.

Documentation has likely been mentioned at least once in every risk management class you have ever attended. The adage was that if it isn't documented it didn't happen. I don't necessarily agree with that and many defense attorneys would, too, but the better the documentation the easier it is for a potential defense expert to follow your thought process when reviewing your care. This is one of the fallacies of electronic records making for a more defensible record: what an electronic record does is force all charts to look similar for patients with similar initial complaints, and they also record what you don't do, too. There was a case where a doctor stated that he had considered each item in each drop down screen of a medical record, but a metadata search by an information technology forensics consultant showed the doctor had spent less than 1/10th of a second on each item, creating the impression the doctor did not actually consider the choices but essentially blew through each one...which may or may not have impacted care, but the technology expert showing the doctor was less-than-honest with his answer did not help him in front of the jury.

In terms of not letting the patient drive the treatment plan, you want a combination of compliant or adherent patients who also "partner" with you in the treatment of the condition at issue. But you are the doctor and the jury will look to you as the person who should be directing care. If you let the patient dictate care, even though there are times when this is good medicine, it gives the patient the opportunity to claim that the you should not have listened, should not have done what the patient wanted; as you are the doctor, you have more knowledge, education, and training than the patient. A jury will readily agree with this.

I once worked on a claim where every defense expert we sought had essentially the same response: *"I know exactly what this doctor was thinking, I likely would have done the same thing, I am sure glad I am not him, but I cannot defend his care."* What happened?

A 34-year-old engineer, earning a six-figure salary and with four children under the age of five, presented to the emergency room complaining of shortness of breath and chest tightness, rapid breathing and heart rate, and a nonproductive cough. The patient stated that he was allergic to long-haired cats, that he had recently spent six days visiting his brother who had long-haired cats, and this reaction was probably from that visit. The ER physician concurred, but called in a pulmonologist for a second opinion. After examining the patient and listening to the patient's story, the pulmonologist gave him a prescription to treat the allergic reaction and sent the patient on his way with documented instructions to call his office or return to the emergency room if his symptoms did not improve within 48 hours.

The symptoms did not improve and the patient did not return to the emergency room until he was brought in dead on arrival four days later. Why could the defense experts not defend the care of the pulmonologist and the emergency room physician? Because the patient essentially presented with a classic presentation of a pulmonary embolism, which is what eventually killed him four days later. But both the emergency room physician and the pulmonologist leaned on the patient's story of being exposed to his brother's long-haired cats and missed what likely would have been their first diagnosis, the pulmonary embolism, but for the cat story.

The patient drove the care that was rendered, no defense experts could be found, and the case had to be settled for a significant amount due to the patient's young age, income and occupation, and young children.

Alternative Dispute Resolution

I have mentioned both mediation and Alternative Dispute Resolution, and using these interchangeably can be misleading. For this I apologize. Alternative Dispute

.

Resolution ("ADR") is a form of resolving disputes that affords the opportunity to take the dispute out of the courtroom and seek to resolve it in a less contentious manner. Mediation is one form of ADR. As noted previously, litigation is nasty, there must be a winner and loser, and the fact that there is a jury involved not only means finding ways to reduce medical terminology to terms a jury can understand but also can bring into play theatrics that can heighten your emotions and distress. I have some personal experience with this and it is extremely difficult and stressful to have to sit in a chair and listen to someone make negative comments about you, especially if the comments are not true or accurate and you must wait to get the truth out...and then hope the jury can discern which version is accurate.

ADR can reduce or eliminate a lot of this stress. There are three basic types of ADR: mediation; arbitration; and, binding arbitration. Mediation is the most common form of ADR and is frequently used in medical and dental malpractice cases. There are two key things to remember about mediation. **First,** both parties should go to mediation expecting a settlement and the only question is the amount and if both parties can agree on the amount. If one party goes to a mediation expecting to be exonerated that person is going for the wrong reason.

Second, one reason mediation is effective is that it starts, and often ends, with both parties face-to-face. Rather than attorneys acting as mouthpieces for the litigants, mediation can get the two parties, who once upon a time were likely on friendly terms, talking to each other as human beings. I attended a mediation once where the allegation was a missed diagnosis of a brain tumor that had metastasized. The patient was a long-term patient of the physician. The patient and his wife were given the opportunity to verbalize the impact this event had on their lives. The defense attorney did a brilliant job of pointing out one very important fact and it is a challenge with any claim involving radiology: things can always be seen in hindsight. The defense attorney presented an x-ray that showed where the tumor was located. He then went back two years to an x-ray that had been taken at a large university medical center and was able to show the patient and his wife that the tumor had been present then, just smaller and more difficult to appreciate. The large university medical center had not only missed it but missed it at a time when treatment would have resulted in a more positive prognosis.

When both sides fully understood the other side, they could come to a settlement both sides could live with. It is often said a good mediation results in both parties being unhappy; this is not always the case.

Another advantage to mediation is the ability to determine any side issues that may have be holding up progress. In one mediation, I was involved with it turned out the patient was interested in being compensated, but also wanted an apology. The doctor refused to apologize as he insisted he had done nothing wrong. At mediation, this became a sticking point until the defense attorney asked the doctor if he regretted what had happened. The doctor said that he certainly did regret what had happened, but that he had done nothing wrong. When it was communicated to the patient what the doctor was willing to say the logjam was broken: across the table the doctor said he regretted what had happened, the patient

.

and doctor shook hands, and the mediation came to a successful conclusion.

A second type of ADR is arbitration. Arbitration is closer to actual litigation than mediation, but still not as contentious. In arbitration, an arbitrator or panel is selected to hear the facts of the case. The arbitrator may be a retired judge or someone else with a legal background, or someone registered and recognized as an arbitrator. Both sides must agree on who the arbitrator will be. If it is a panel it may be composed of people with legal and/or medical backgrounds; usually one side selects one person, the other side selects one person, and those two people select a third member of the panel.

In arbitration evidence is presented, just as at a trial. Expert witnesses may be called or their deposition testimony placed into evidence. There will be opening statements, evidence presented, and closing statements. The arbitrator or panel will then study all the evidence, exhibits, expert testimony, etc. and render a decision, perhaps in a couple of hours or it may take a few days for everything to be reviewed and the arbitrators to discuss the case.

Two key differences between a jury trial and arbitration is that there is, or course, no jury; this can take the theatrics out of the case. Second, the arbitrator or panel will want facts only, along with expert opinions, so the setting tends to be less contentious.

Once a ruling is handed down one or both sides can reject it and move on to a jury trial, while perhaps using information gleaned from the arbitration hearing to discuss a settlement. It would be considered bad faith to agree to arbitration solely to learn the arguments of the other side, but it does happen.

The third type of ADR is binding arbitration and it is as it sounds: the same process as arbitration, but the ruling of the arbitrator or panel is final, both sides must accept it.

One thing to remember about all forms of ADR; they occur AFTER discovery has occurred, so there will still be interrogatories, subpoenas, and likely depositions before one side or the other suggests ADR.

One BIG advantage to ADR speaks directly to one reason you are prone to litigation stress and often would prefer to settle rather than defend at trial: **publicity**. If word of the filing of the claim gets out, and it surely will, you will be concerned about your family and about the impact on staff. Address the issue with staff, with guidance from your attorney and/or company claims adjuster; they will help guide you through the challenge of talking about the claim without talking about the claim, talking about the fact that a claim has been filed, which is the right of any citizen under the Constitution, without going into details about the care and jeopardizing defense of the claim. You will also want a "spin phrase," a pat statement from either your attorney or your insurance company that all staff, including you, will use if any patients ask about the case. Someone may have told them about it, they may have read about it in the paper, and it is this fear of dealing with patients concerning the existence of a malpractice claim that adds to the stress of litigation. Preparing for it, being in CONTROL to the extent you can be, helps reduce distress.

You can't deny the existence of the claim: if a legal suit has been filed anyone can go down to the courthouse and get a copy of it. And one very frustrating part is that an attorney can put anything they want to in a law suit, regardless of how accurate or true it is. Why? Because they don't have to prove it until they get in front of a jury and by then, through the discovery process, the suit will change two or three times, maybe more.

Is this ethical? Not according to the laws of most states and ethical guidelines put forth by the American Bar Association and most state Bar Associations. It is lying under oath and should constitute contempt of court. But courts rarely punish it and, in the interim, you and your staff, and maybe your family, must deal with what is in the suit papers and you need to be prepared ahead of time with stock answers that get you past the situation quickly and with as little stress as possible.

A great example of this was a case many years ago, in a major metropolitan area, a huge case involving six doctors and three hospitals. Both local papers and the local television stations covered it. On the day the case was sent to the jury both papers and all the TV stations were there to cover the verdict live. The jury returned a unanimous verdict for the **defense.** Not a dime changed hands. Regardless of whether justice was done or not there was nary a word of the verdict on TV or in the papers. It was dog bites man, not man bites dog. No money, no story.

Excellent preparation by you and your attorney, with input from your insurance company, will prepare you to deal with these distractions, minimize harm to your practice, and help reduce your levels of distress.

Interrogatories and subpoenas

As noted, the primary purpose of discovery is learning what the other side knows and what information it has, and a large part of this information is obtained via interrogatories and subpoenas. Interrogatories are questions or requests for information that each side propounds on the other side. Part of the legal jousting that occurs, one of the things that takes this beyond the scientific inquiry a doctor would like, is in what questions are asked, how they are asked, how many are asked, what documents are requested and what is relevant. Normally if a question is not deemed to be relevant to the facts of the case an attorney will object to the question being asked, direct you to answer the question, then object to the question or answer when it comes time to go before a judge.

This process can be tedious, burdensome, exhausting, and nasty. You should prepare to be asked anything and everything, and then leave it to your attorney to object as necessary. While rare in a malpractice case, you may be asked the same question or have the same documents requested multiple times; when this occurs, your attorney should object, but in the case I was personally involved in the other side used five different law firms and 18 different attorneys over four years, who all asked the same questions and requested the same documents, over and over. What they were really looking for was a document showing up in response to one request that did not show up in a similar request, or vice versa. This is used to allegedly show you are deceptive.

If something is requested in an interrogatory it will be requested with the use of a subpoena or subpoena duces tecum. A subpoena is issued by the court, or by an attorney as an officer of the court, to order someone to be present at a certain time and place to present testimony related to a legal matter. This is usually used to set up a time and location for someone to be deposed.

A subpoena duces tecum is properly used to request documents or other physical evidence to be sent to the court or to opposing counsel as an officer of the court. For example, today opposing counsel will routinely subpoena emails, medical records, memos, phone logs, meeting notes, and anything else that may yield useful information for the case. In theory, there are some items that should be out-of-bounds as being irrelevant and it will be up to your attorney to object to any subpoena not judged to be relevant, but the courts grant great leeway in allowing documents and other items to be subpoenaed. For example, it is not out-of-bounds to request blood samples, blood test information, medical bills and insurance information, income tax returns, photographs, and even employment history and records.

Originally the proper use of either a subpoena or subpoena duces tecum was to assist an attorney in obtaining information to help prove or disprove a case, but this has been broadened by precedent setting cases over the years to where almost anything can be subpoenaed, just on the chance something might be found. Big Dawg law firms are usually given more leeway than small firms and solo attorneys. Where the legal jousting comes in is in determining where the parameters of that information reside. For example, is it relevant for the plaintiff's attorney to ask for all your medical records for your entire life if you are a doctor defending yourself against a malpractice claim? It would be up to your attorney to fight something such as this unless you feel as if you have nothing to hide. On the other hand, asking for the plaintiff's medical, dental, and even counseling records is a routine request to see if any information was withheld from the provider or if anything not reported to the provider contributed to the outcome in any way.

But strange twists and turns can occur in litigation and sometimes karma can bite someone at the wrong time. Several years ago, a surgeon was being deposed for a malpractice case and he asked to take a break in the deposition. Outside he drank a couple of glasses of water and said he was ready to go back into the deposition. When asked why he needed a break he said that he had a minor seizure disorder that sometimes occurred when he became dehydrated, he could feel it coming on, and it was going to occur in the room where the deposition was being held. He and the attorney returned, the physician completed the deposition, end of story, correct?

Not really.

When the defense attorney phoned in the report of the deposition to the claims handler for the insurance company she mentioned the hydration break. The claims person then reviewed the surgeon's application for insurance and noted that he had not listed the seizure disorder on the application. Based on this the insurance company tried to walk away from defending the claim, even though no aspect of the claim was related to the seizure disorder or to the surgeon having a seizure. The surgeon sued both the attorney and the company for bad faith and won, as the application asked about "...material physical, mental, or emotional disorders..." that would prevent the applicant from performing the duties of his profession. It was the position of the surgeon, as a physician, that as the seizure disorder was rare, mild, under control, he could determine if something was going to happen and it did not happen if he stayed hydrated, it was not a "material" physical disorder. He won and the company had to defend the claim (after which it non-renewed his policy), but for the time that he was without coverage it meant there was no money for the plaintiff attorney to pursue, no insurance money, so the claim was non-suited until the bad faith case was settled.

Depositions

Rightly or wrongly, a deposition can make or break a case. For you as the defendant it is your best opportunity to impress the plaintiff's attorney with your demeanor, ability to clearly articulate your answers which may sometimes be complex or technical, and your ability to stay cool under fire. And by "cool" I mean it literally as more than one attorney has been known to turn up the heat in a deposition room and place the deponent under a duct. Frequently the duct is also located near a very bright ceiling light that produces a lot of heat. And today it is quite typical for attorneys, especially defense attorneys with virtually unlimited funds at their disposal, to record the deposition, but not the whole deposition: if your deposition is recorded the camera will be trained solely on you from about mid-chest on up, a very tight frame. This places more pressure on you as you are supposed to sit still, to stay in the frame, and look directly into the camera when you answer. The longer a deposition drags on, the more uncomfortable you can become and the more often you should ask for a break.

When you add up the heat, bright lights, camera, and having to sit very still it places you in a very awkward position and that is intentional. Very important: you can ask for and must be given a break anytime you ask for one, so don't be afraid to ask frequently. If opposing counsel objects, have your attorney tell him/her to turn down the heat, turn off the light, and/or pull the camera back so you can sit more comfortably.

According to the Ethics of the American Bar Association a deposition is supposed to be about fact finding, the opposing counsel asking questions about the case to gain information for use at trial. Unfortunately, our legal system has devolved to where today an attorney can and will ask you anything. Legal articles have been written about "Rambo-style" lawyering. The deposition will start with "softball" questions to establish who you are, your age, where you practice, your specialty, where you went to school, marital status, and the like. These questions are designed to get some basic information on the record, but also designed to get you to relax and start talking freely. Stay relaxed, but see the rules for depositions below and you will note talking freely is not on the list. Then the attorney will ask a series of questions that are either irrelevant to the case or largely irrelevant to the case, some of the questions personal, some insulting, all designed to get you riled up before getting to the questions that are the "meat" of the deposition. The hope is that in an agitated state you will blurt out answers that are not really accurate or appear hostile, and all of this is recorded on camera and can be shown to the jury. For example, a case I was involved in resulted in me being deposed over two days and for over 12 hours; the entire first day of questioning only contained maybe four questions that directly related to the case and they were softball questions, while the balance of the questions were asked solely to tire me out and agitate me. This is not supposed to happen and did not when attorneys took their positions as "officers of the court" seriously; today, however, attorneys are trained to win and to win at all costs for their clients, so out of 12 hours there might only be a dozen questions that really matter to the case, but your behavior may be a bigger issue.

Which brings me to the "rules" you should follow when being deposed. These are general rules and you should always follow the advice and training given to you by the team representing you, but your attorney should give you instructions like the following:

1. Listen carefully to the question being asked and make sure you understand it. If you don't understand it or if it is not worded correctly, state that you cannot answer the question as asked and ask that it be repeated in a different manner. Don't help with the question!

2. Once you believe you understand the question that is being asked, pause for three or four seconds to develop your answer before giving it and be consistent in this pause for each question, even if the answer is going to be "yes" or "no." This pause not only gives you time to truly think about the question and answer, it also gives your attorney time to object to the question being

asked if he/she thinks it is irrelevant, has already been asked and answered, or for any other reason wants to object to the question. By objecting at the time the question is being asked it gives your attorney the ability to ask the court to eliminate it from any future proceeding, including at trial. If you don't allow your attorney to object at the time the question is asked it becomes more difficult to get the answer discarded in the future.

3. When you answer the question, speak slowly and distinctly, and only answer the question that is being asked. Doctors love to teach; don't teach with your answer. If a question is phrased wrong, don't correct opposing counsel so it can be asked correctly, just state that you are unable to answer the question as it is asked. What do I mean by only answering the question that is being asked and not giving too much information? The best example I have ever heard was from an episode of the television show "The West Wing" where the president's wife was going to be deposed and the counsel assigned to her was preparing her for the deposition. At one point he asks, "Do you have the time?" The First Lady responded, "It's 9:15." Her attorney said, "**That is the habit I need to break you of, giving more information than is asked for.**" Go back and read the question again if you don't get this point. The correct answer is "yes" or "no."

4. Don't try to answer multiple questions disguised as one question, a common tactic of attorneys trying to force you into muddled or poor answers.

117

.

If you are asked two or three questions disguised as one question, state so to the attorney and tell him you cannot answer the question as asked. If he asks why not, it is not considered to be helping the attorney if you tell him there were two or three questions rolled into one and that you cannot answer unless the questions are separated.

5. In the "old days" before recorded depositions there was only the transcript of the deposition for people to go by. The printed word does not pick up nuance, manner, facial expressions, and the like. With recorded depositions, it is now quite easy for an attorney to play back for the jury an answer that shows your facial expression, picks up any exasperation or anger in your voice, allows the jury to hear you hesitate mid-answer (which may mean you are trying to find the right words or it might come off as being evasive), or the like. This underscores the importance of not only pausing before answering, to understand the question, formulate your answer (even if it is a one-word answer), and to allow your attorney time to object, it also gives you time to collect yourself, ask for a break, get a drink of water, order a sandwich, or whatever else you need to do to stay calm, cool and collected during the deposition.

6. After opposing counsel is done your attorney may or may not have questions for you. If your attorney has questions opposing counsel may have additional questions afterwards. In one deposition I was in there were five defendants and I was testifying solely as an expert in professional

118

liability insurance, not as a fact witness; each attorney got their turn with me, then got a second turn with me after the first round, and a promised 45-minute deposition turned into four hours. And the case settled! It never even went to trial!

After the deposition, all attorneys will be given the opportunity to review a copy of the transcript to make sure it is accurate and you may be asked to review it to make sure the court reporter accurately captured your answers. If this occurs, make sure you read it carefully and that your answers were accurately captured. One minor item that you may be best equipped to correct is misspelled names and words.

The most important thing to remember is that a deposition is your best opportunity to derail a case before trial. If your answers are solid and your demeanor calm, cool and collected it sends a clear message to opposing counsel that the case must be won on merit and not on you doing a poor job on the stand. However, if your deposition does not go well it is not the end of the world as you can still correct things on the stand if the case gets as far as a jury. The only challenge at that point, especially if you give contradictory answers, will be in convincing the jury that the incorrect answer was a mistake, the answer on the stand is correct, and that the incorrect answer was an honest mistake, a statement made in the heat of the moment.

Some attorneys will really work hard to obtain relevant facts concerning the case, while others will meander all over the place, asking irrelevant questions (which is why you wait to answer, so your attorney can object based on relevancy) and then interjecting a relevant question every now and then. Honest, emotional response? These are the attorneys I would like to punch in the throat. They will drag depositions on for hours, with only a few minutes seemingly devoted to obtaining relevant information. What they are doing is trying to lull you into becoming complacent and then ask you a question that suddenly requires your complete attention, which they hope has been distracted by the questions up to that point. They may also ask questions, some relevant, some not, that they hope will elicit contradictory statements, either contradictory to any interrogatories (written answers) you have provided, previous statements by you, or documents obtained by other means.

For example, an attorney may harp on your record in medical school, during internship and residency, and during any fellowship years. He may read down the list of every class listed on your transcript and ask for the grade you earned in that class; if you answered that you received a B+ in organic chemistry and you really received a C- the attorney may take you to task there, in order to harass you, distract you, get under your skin, and hopefully get you agitated enough to snap off bad answers; or, the attorney may wait and spring this on you in front of the jury to question your credibility, your honesty, your ability to recall events, etc., all in an effort to make you look shifty in front of the jury. Your attorney will or should object and should point out that your transcript says what your transcript says, the relevant point is that you graduated from medical school.

By the way, if an attorney has a copy of your transcript and starts asking about it, ask your attorney if you can simply say that you will agree with whatever is on the transcript, assuming it is a certified copy of the transcript.

Also, if you get as far as a jury trial or even ADR you may be asked a question that is similar to one that you were asked in deposition, but not identical. In a case in which I was involved I was asked a question one way in deposition and answered the question based on how it was asked, then asked a similar question in front of the jury, responded differently, and the defense attorney jumped on my inconsistent answers. I was very fortunate in that I could recall the deposition question, I told the defense attorney I had just answered differently from the way I had in deposition because he had asked a different question. At that point he went back to his table, dramatically pulled a copy of the deposition, then asked the question that was asked in the deposition, and I responded the way I had in deposition. While I doubt if this little sideshow made the case, I was fortunate in remembering the question from the deposition, was fortunate I noted he had asked it differently, and was fortunate that opposing counsel had the deposition transcript and was essentially forced to ask the question a second time and get a different answer. I believe it went a long way in developing my credibility in front of the jury and calling into question the credibility or competence of opposing counsel and, by relationship, his clients and their case.

And that last point needs to be emphasized a little bit so that you are prepared. You are the client of the defense team assigned to defend you; the plaintiff, your former patient, is the client of the plaintiff's attorney or team the patient selected to represent him or her. After

121

.

that it becomes the litigation of the attorneys and in a very real sense you are a "prop" in the litigation. A very important prop, but a prop all the same. Or as an attorney said to me during a trial (in the hallway, not in front of the jury), "Don't screw up MY litigation." Except he used a different word than "screw," but point made.

At each step of the discovery process, from documents to experts to depositions, information will be gathered by both sides that will enable them to start to form an opinion on the claim and the approach to take. Settlement offers may be proffered at any time and each attorney has a duty to report the opportunity to the client. Your attorney will recommend accepting or declining the offer and you should follow the lead of your attorney. In addition, as noted, during the discovery phase is when expert witnesses will be developed. Once the discovery phase is nearing its end if good expert witnesses have been found on your behalf the decision will likely be made to continue defending the case; as noted in my claim example concerning long-haired cats, if defense experts cannot be found a case will likely become a settlement candidate.

Trial

OK, let's say you have been served with suit papers, a formal claim has been started, all necessary affidavits have been obtained, you have answered interrogatories and responded to subpoenas, you have been deposed, you have deposed the plaintiff, both sides have developed and deposed expert and fact witnesses, settlement offers may or may not have been made: what is left? **A jury trial**! And it will be a jury trial because while you will not

122

be truly tried by a jury of your peers (other doctors) jurors are not asked to assess law, they are only asked to assess right and wrong, good and bad, and in the case of a malpractice case, if you were negligent. So, the plaintiff will always demand a jury trial, rather than a bench trial with just the judge deciding the case, while the defense will try to get the case dismissed before trial.

But let's say you're going to trial. What should you expect?

First, don't expect most of the trial to be like what you see on television unless you happen to watch a trial from beginning to end on Court TV or the like. Judge Judy? Judge Joe Brown? That is actual justice being dispensed. Watching these shows on TV people are misled into thinking the legal system is about justice. It is not. The legal system is all about the legal system; ironically Judge Judy and Judge Joe Brown are about justice because their cases are based solely on the facts, right and wrong, good and bad. No high-priced lawyers citing case law and trying to confuse witnesses, the court, or the jury. Just the facts, as used to be said on the television show "Dragnet." (Note: if you are under 30 you can find Dragnet on either Me TV or Antenna TV). These TV shows are the closest thing to actual justice our civil legal system has to offer, two opposing people presenting just the facts and a judge assessing right and wrong, good and bad. The actual civil legal system has largely devolved into something far removed from anything remotely resembling justice, I am sorry to say. This stark realization for me was staggering, that more real justice occurs at the civil level on TV shows than in real life.

I will later talk about physical and emotional fitness as a means of helping deal with litigation stress; physical and emotional fitness will also help you through a jury trial. Part of the reason for this is that a jury trial is quite similar to how your claim has worked its way up to the jury trial; bursts of activity intermixed with periods of tedium and boredom for you. But during these periods it is still essential that you pay attention to everything that is going on and to write down questions and thoughts to later discuss with your attorney. Therefore, physical and emotional fitness is important.

Know this about attorneys, especially litigators: **they are trained from their first interaction with someone to try and determine what the worst thing is that a person can do to them, and to immediately start determining and put into action things that can be done to prevent this from happening**. Sounds like a stressful way to live your life? This is why so few attorneys are litigators. I will not state that all litigators are psychopaths or sociopaths or narcissists, I am not qualified to do so; but to do what they do for a living it certainly is helpful to have some of those traits. Remember that sociopaths, narcissists, and psychopaths tend not to look at people as human beings but as" things" to be used; therefore, you may find yourself in litigation that is intensely personal and draining to you, but the attorneys will refer to it as "their" litigation. You are just the object that the litigation is about.

Sound cold? It is, but it is also necessary to help the attorney keep a level head, even demeanor, and clear eyes. I have sat next to a fulltime litigator during hearings and a trial, and I am convinced a bomb could go off under

124

his chair and he would not feel or hear it, so intense is the concentration on every word. Why? Because opposing counsel is out to win in any way possible, ethics, morals, right and wrong be damned, and losing is the worst thing for litigators, so they are trying to prevent that "worst thing" from happening.

The tedium for you starts with the very first minutes of the very first day, when the judge and opposing counsel deal with various "housekeeping" issues, including last minute motions, objections, appeals, and the like. If opposing counsel have agreed on one consistent set of jury instructions (highly unlikely) they may present it to the judge at this time; more likely, each side will have more differences than similarities when it comes to jury instructions and so each side will present to the judge what they would like the jury instructions to be, the judge will take both sets under advisement, and the judge will then develop a single set of jury instructions to be given to the jury at the close of evidence. Either side can object to certain jury instructions, usually based on precedent case law, and the judge can either note the objection or can make a change to the jury instruction. Once a case has been heard, the instructions read to the jury, and the jury retires to try and reach a verdict, it is usually too late and a violation of civil procedure for either side to then object to one or more jury instructions and very poor form to object after a verdict has been arrived at...unless the losing side expects to lose and keeps the objection in its back pocket to be used as part of any appeal.

Which is a nice way of saying that in the American civil justice system, it ain't over even after it's over.

Once the housekeeping is dispensed with the judge will formally ask for any last-minute objections or appeals, but these issues should have long been dispensed with and the judge will likely deny them. The judge will then order the bailiff to bring in the available jury pool for that day, usually between 30-45 people. The judge will briefly discuss the basic facts of the case with the entire pool and ask some general questions in an attempt to eliminate certain jurors who either believe they could not be impartial or who the court believes could not be impartial. This could be because someone is married to or otherwise related to a health care practitioner or may even be a health care practitioner, it could be because the person has been involved personally or closely with someone who was involved in a malpractice case, or it could be because a person admits to certain prejudices against either health care providers or towards people trying to "win the lottery" by suing health care providers and driving up the cost of health care.

Then, usually in groups of six to 12 people at a time, the attorneys, will try to select the jurors they would like to hear the case, based on the brief biographical sketch made available to them. This process is called *voir dire.*

In the United States, it now generally refers to the process by which prospective jurors are questioned about their backgrounds and potential biases before being chosen to sit on a jury. But it also can refer to other decisions the court must make concerning a trial that are usually heard outside the hearing of the jury, such as the process by which expert witnesses are questioned about their backgrounds and qualifications before being allowed to present their opinion testimony in court. In the United

·

States (especially under the Federal Rules of Evidence which may differ from the Rules of Evidence in each state), *voir dire* can also refer to examination of the background of a witness to assess their qualification or fitness to give testimony on a given subject.

In *voir dire,* each side can deselect a certain number of jurors. The key, the combination of science and art, is to not run out of your chances to deselect too quickly, leaving the other side to "stack the deck" with jurors it thinks and hopes will be sympathetic to its side. In a huge case with massive potential damages, usually between two massive corporations, attorneys will bring in alleged jury experts to help select the jury and to observe the jury during the trial, so they can help direct an attorney towards a juror they might be "losing." This is not a routine matter in a medical malpractice case as these cases are so much more fact-oriented than other cases, but don't be surprised if jury experts show up to help select the jury and to monitor the jury during the trial.

Once a jury is seated there will be some other housekeeping matters addressed, another slate of routine objections will be heard and, usually, dismissed, and the judge will then go into more detail about the case with the jury and render some admonitions to them concerning discussing the case outside of the courtroom or with any third parties. Then, after as much as one entire day, the actual trial will commence.

A trial starts with opening statements and ends with closing statements in a specific order: the plaintiff goes first with opening statements and the defense goes first with closing statements. For opening statements the plaintiff goes first to, in a manner of speaking, "set the table," then the defense gets to counter with what it plans to show in terms of you having done everything possible for the patient and that no one could have rendered better care. For closing arguments, the order is reversed with your defense attorney speaking first, in an attempt to convince the jury that it did show what it said it would show, and that you as the defendant did NOT render care below the prevailing standard of care, that your care was not negligent. The plaintiff gets to wrap up with a closing that will basically be just the opposite of what your attorney said, highlighting points its expert(s) made, if they were strong, and/or trying to send the jury off to deliberate with an emotional appeal to the jury, assuming the injured party has been portrayed as someone who has suffered much.

During the trial the plaintiff will go first, putting on witnesses both fact and expert, including the actual plaintiff if the attorney feels that he/she will make a good witness. During this time the plaintiff's expert witnesses will testify as to why their opinion is that your care fell below the acceptable standard; with the help of you, your records and your expert witnesses your attorney will be prepared to attempt to discredit or poke holes in the testimony of any expert witness. Your attorney will be allowed to cross-examine these plaintiff's witnesses.

Under the heading of "it takes all kinds" the plaintiff may hire what is called a "hired gun" expert witness, physicians who spend more time testifying (sometimes for only plaintiffs, sometimes for whoever pays them the most money) than practicing medicine. If this is the case your attorney will likely spend some time trying to create doubt in the minds of the jurors about how deeply held the convictions are of this expert, given that he or she is paid large sums of money to fly all over the country testifying. However, this should be done with some care as in the past some juries have looked at this "hired gun" status as a good thing; the logic is that this expert must be someone special if he/she gets paid hundreds of thousands of dollars each year to fly around the country and testify at trials.

After the plaintiff has rested his/her case it will be your turn and you may be chomping at the bit at this point, after listening to all the negative things that may have been said about you. You may be angry or you may be depressed. What you wanted was a scientific inquiry and what you got instead was likely theater.

This is a good time to dial it down, to relax, and to use some of the relaxation techniques described in a later chapter of this book. Just as you should not go into a deposition angry, you don't want to take the witness stand angry…if you take the witness stand at all. Your attorney will likely want you on the witness stand, will want you to stand up and defend the care that you rendered. After all is said and done, especially by the plaintiff, the jury will want to hear from you.

Would there be a reason to not put you on the stand? Yes. One is that the facts of the case speak for themselves and your attorney feels there is no need to put you on the stand and subject you to cross-examination by the plaintiff's attorney. The other reason, more common, is the fear that you will not make a good witness on your own behalf…which again brings us back to being able to keep a normal stress level from reaching distress. After much coaching and cheerleading and fact-finding and logical thinking, you may still feel unprepared to take the stand on your own behalf and your attorney and company claims person likely will see that. Most companies today offer a lot of pre-trial coaching, taking you through the questions you will be asked by your attorney and the expected questions that the plaintiff's attorney will ask you. Every effort will be made in practice to rattle you; the better you can deal with this in practice the better you will be able to deal with this at trial.

Keep in mind, too, that after you have finished responding to the questions from the plaintiff's attorney your attorney will be able to question you again or help clarify something you said on the stand that the jury may be confused about because of the way you answered a question from the plaintiff. This is called a "re-direct."

As I am writing this I am writing it very dispassionately. If you have never been involved in a malpractice claim, you are likely reading it dispassionately. If you are involved in a claim as we speak you may be taking notes on questions you want answered. As I will note in the epilogue at the end of this book, staying dispassionate when someone is trying to rattle you is difficult. Now consider that the person trying to rattle you is trained to do so and experienced at doing so, that this person makes a living trying to get under the skin of other people and make them lose control. I am writing this dispassionately but when you are in the middle of it, as I will discuss from personal experience, it can be very difficult to keep from losing control of your emotions, both at deposition and at trial. This can be especially difficult when the opposing counsel twists your words, written or oral, and completely makes up the reason or reasons why you took a specific action, and you know the truth.

What can help? Being prepared ahead of time AND constantly reminding yourself that this attorney, who is only doing his/her job (I know, the "Nazi Defense") WANTS you to lose it, that they are working hard to get you to lose it, and so **I want you to be prepared to be able to vow that you will not give this attorney the satisfaction of getting you to lose control of your emotions, either in front of the jury or at deposition. You must vow and then prepare yourself to stay above any attempts to get you to lose control**. You may not experience this at all. The plaintiff's attorney may be above-board and only focus on the facts of the case (which would include things such as your training, education, work experience, perhaps past claims if they are relevant, but not your hobbies, number of ex-spouses, sexual proclivities, number of traffic tickets, and the like).

Depending on the damages and complexity of the case there may only be a handful of witnesses, fact and expert, over a two or three-day trial. If the case is complex with multiple defendants, there could be dozens of witnesses asked to testify and the trial could last one week or longer. On the witness stand the most amount of time will be spent with you, the plaintiff, and the expert witnesses; most other witnesses will be fact witnesses supporting one side or the other, along with witnesses that speak to the impact of the alleged malpractice.

And I specifically use "alleged" because until a jury examines all the facts and states that you were in fact negligent, any allegation of malpractice is just that, an allegation. One of the more frustrating things about our

131

legal system is that in suit papers and other motions either side can put in not only outrageous statements but can include actual lies. I won't sugarcoat it and use phrases such as "inaccurate statements" or "statements lacking in merit" or, more recently, "alternative facts." People do not understand that ANYTHING can be said in a lawsuit, but it does not have to be supported, it does not have to be proven, unless and until you get in front of a jury.

This may strike you as absurd, as you may have believed as I did for years that the legal system was designed to get to the truth and deliver justice. You may have believed, as I did, that the first duty of any lawyer is to the court and the legal system, and therefore to truth and facts that can be supported. You may well have believed, as I did, that an attorney has an ethical obligation to **not** move forward with a fraudulent case. **These things I believed and they are _not_ true.**

I will tell you that a lawyer's first obligation today is to his/client, truth or facts be damned. Does any Bar Association, American or state, have guidelines for ethical conduct that would preclude some of the actions in the preceding paragraph? Yes. Are they enforced? Rarely. Why? Because most lawyers are reluctant to ask for sanctions, against either opposing counsel or their clients, for two primary reasons: first, payback is hell; second, any attorney is cautioned to not seek sanctions unless the actions are extremely egregious, professional courtesy or whatever you want to call it.

The only attorneys who routinely ask for sanctions are corporate defense attorneys, those attorneys who earn $400 to $600 per hour usually defending behavior that is indefensible. What I have learned and experienced is that these attorneys routinely threaten and ask for sanctions as a means of *intimidation*. It is a part of their legal strategy. Is this ethical? I will tell you that Bar Association ethics do state that the repeated use or threat of sanctions, especially when unwarranted and as part of an ongoing and repeated pattern used to threaten and intimidate is itself worthy of sanctions. Does it happen? Rarely, especially if an attorney belongs to a Big Dawg firm. That is not to say it has never happened, but in modern times it is rare.

You may ask why, if your attorney won't ask for sanctions, can you not go to the State Bar and ask for disciplinary action against the opposing attorney? The likely response, the one I received when I attempted this with documented, extreme justification, was **that I was only allowed to complain about the conduct of my attorney, not the conduct of opposing counsel**. To ask that opposing counsel be disciplined first requires the court to sanction the attorney and, as noted above, apart from corporate defense attorneys who routinely use the threat of sanctions as a litigation tool, as well as their corporate clients who use litigation as part of their business strategy, attorneys are loathe to ask for sanctions against opposing counsel.

There was a case in the Western United States a couple of years ago, where an attorney spent the better part of six hours asking question after question completely irrelevant to the case. The deponent's attorney objected to each question based on relevance. But then the issue was brought to the attention of the state Bar Association which then disciplined **BOTH** attorneys, the attorney who asked all the irrelevant questions for doing just that, making a mockery of the legal system, obstructing justice, and abusing the discovery process; but that State Bar also disciplined the attorney for the person being deposed, although less severely, for not reporting the first attorney to the Bar Association.

Unfortunately, actions such as these, where the wrongdoing of an attorney is punished, are very rare. Essentially an attorney must either mishandle money or commit and be convicted of an overt criminal act before any State Bar Association will act, and if the attorney is with a large firm there is even less chance of the proper punishment being meted out (refer to Gladwell's "Principles of Legitimacy"). In the case of both attorneys being sanctioned, that State Bar is to be applauded; in most states the Bar would take no action.

While the longer a trial proceeds the more difficult this may become, PAY ATTENTION to the witnesses. As much as both legal teams know about the case, **you know more than anyone**. Any misstatements or inaccurate facts need to be written down by you and communicated to your attorney so that corrections can be made, witnesses recalled, and the most accurate information presented to the jury. No one is supposed to knowingly present false information to a court, but especially on the corporate-side of the law this is routine. Someone can lie by omission or commission, by what they don't say or what they do say. What corporate attorneys are good at doing is presenting partial facts, lying by omission, to present a one-sided, but incomplete, picture to the court and, if it is allowed, to the jury. Your attention to the testimony of others is crucial as you know more than anyone else. If misinformation is presented, by

134

omission or commission, make sure your attorney gets the correct facts into the record. And don't let your attorney tell you it is irrelevant; what may be irrelevant to an attorney could be extremely relevant to the lay person sitting on the jury who will decide the case.

At trial once both sides have concluded their cases they will present closing arguments to the jury. As noted previously, at closing the defense will go first and will usually try to convince the jury that it was shown you were not negligent, something occurred, it was unfortunate what happened to the patient, but that you were not negligent. Then the plaintiff's attorney will close with just the opposite argument, that negligence clearly and convincingly did occur, that this was shown to the jury quite clearly, and that based on a preponderance of the evidence you (and any co-defendants) should be found to have committed negligence with a commensurate award to the injured plaintiff. Whichever side had the strongest expert witnesses will play up their testimony.

Note that I used the phrase "...*based on a preponderance of the evidence*." As mentioned previously, this is not a criminal trial. In criminal cases, which we tend to be more familiar with due to television shows, the bar is set at a verdict being rendered based on evidence showing guilt "beyond a reasonable doubt." That is a higher bar to hurdle than a "preponderance of the evidence." It is one reason, for example, how one jury in the O.J. Simpson case, the criminal trial, found Simpson not guilty of murder, while in the civil suit that was filed by the family of Nicole Brown Simpson a jury found that Simpson was negligent in the death of his wife, based on a preponderance of the evidence.

135

Once both closing arguments have been given there will likely be a few more motions made to the judge, some oral discussions held out of earshot of the jury, the defense will likely make a motion that the case be dismissed, the judge will almost assuredly deny the request, and then the jury instructions will be read to the jury and a copy of them given to the jury.

The jury instructions are not a uniform list. As noted, both sides will issue their own list of jury instructions, what they want the jury to consider in rendering a verdict. It will not be the same list. The judge will ask the attorneys if they can reconcile the two lists into one, that answer will likely be no, so the judge will recess the court, adjourn to his/her chambers, and draw up a set of jury instructions, which will then be presented to the attorneys for approval. There may still be discussion of the instructions, but eventually one set of jury instructions will be read to the jury and then given to the jury to use while it deliberates. In a fact-based case such as a medical malpractice suit the jury instructions are usually not as complicated as in a complex business litigation case or a defamation case, where there exists not only actual laws that come into play but also precedent-setting cases that help refine and define the law, but can also be used by both sides to argue their case, making things very complex for a jury.

During deliberations, which could last 20 minutes or could last for a few days depending on facts and the complexity of the case, along with the jury instructions, the jury may ask the court for clarification. Depending on when the case goes to the jury you may be able to leave the courthouse. If deliberations do not render a verdict at the end of a day, the jury will be dismissed for the day with the admonition to not discuss the case with anyone. And this is where problems can occur today.

In the past, it is likely that jurors would go home and discuss the case, but it was likely with spouses or family members. Many would take their civic duty seriously enough that they did not discuss the case at all. Today there have been cases where jurors get on the internet and start researching all parties in a case, look for information on similar cases, and will even visit Facebook and Linked In pages for the parties in a suit, if they can be found (NOTE: I am not on Facebook, I am on Linked In). Where this prejudices the juror is that it takes the juror away from the facts of the case and introduces other information that can be used to reach a verdict. A jury is supposed to render a verdict based on the facts presented in the case before them and nothing else. Biases and experience may influence their thinking, but only the case before them is the case they should be basing their decision on. All this superfluous information can impact their thinking, though it should not.

An example of how this thinking comes into play was a case that ended up being settled in a conservative jurisdiction, before the explosion of the internet and Facebook and Google, etc. A female who had undergone breast augmentation was suing over unsatisfactory results. My physician explained to me the steps he went through before all breast augmentations and showed me where he performed these same steps, including consent, with this patient. It was noted that often there is the need for some additional follow-up work to make the results as aesthetically pleasing as possible.

·

This patient had selected the size cup she wanted to move up to, the procedure had gone well, there was a need for a little revision work to be done, and the doctor believed it was another successful case. So, he was surprised when the patient sent him a letter demanding a full refund as she was not happy with the results, that he had done a poor job, and that she had gone to another plastic surgeon who had to undo and then redo all the previous work.

The case sounded defensible and got more so when we saw the work that had been "re-done" by the second surgeon. Putting it as delicately as possible, the woman had upgraded her implants from, let's say, grapefruit size to basketball size. No exaggeration. At deposition it was determined that the woman's boyfriend, a member of a motor cycle club, had wanted his woman to be much larger than what my doctor had done, they found another surgeon to do the work, and what they really wanted was all the money back from the first procedure to help pay for the second procedure.

More than enough for us to win a jury trial based on the facts, correct? But in all honesty, there was one more thing that made us want to take the case to trial. In the second "after" picture, taken by the second plastic surgeon, you could now see a tattoo coming over the shoulder of the woman with what looked like a dragon's tail extending down between her breasts. And that is what it was, for on her back was the balance of the dragon, with the tail extending over her shoulder and down the front of her body.

Our thinking was simple: in addition to no negligence on the part of our physician and the deposition of the patient, showing these photographs to the typical conservative jury in this jurisdiction was not going to make for a very sympathetic plaintiff. We discussed trying to get as many elderly females on the jury as possible.

The physician, however, elected to settle the case if the woman would dismiss the law suit and he would reimburse her all her money. Why? The physician just did not want to go to a public jury trial in his home town, a town where he grew up, had gone to school, and had then come back to practice after medical school, residency, and fellowship training. In addition, if you pay out of your pocket you do not have to report yourself to the National Practitioner Data Bank (however, you always undertake this type of settlement with the guidance of your malpractice insurance company and the attorney assigned to handle the case for you).

But what relevance does this case have to do with the world we live in today? We discovered all this information the old-fashioned way, through the discovery process. But today people feel compelled to put their entire lives out there for the whole world to see, Facebook, Twitter, Linked In, etc. There is every likelihood that we could have discovered this and much more about this plaintiff in the world we live in today by simply sitting at a computer, and that is the concern whenever a jury is dismissed for the evening or a weekend. A friend of mine who was involved in a defamation case against her former employer found that a couple of jurors did look her up overnight on both Facebook and Linked In, but as there was nothing relevant to the case on either site it was never mentioned to the judge. However, she won at trial, as she should have; her former employer had massively

.

defamed her, ruined her reputation, and made it impossible for her to find a job in her chosen profession. Her employer just never figured she would fight back and, when she did, the jury took the facts and rendered the correct decision. As I have mentioned repeatedly, if a case gets to a jury trial the jurors are just asked to assess right and wrong, not apply the law, and jurors get it right most of the time. However, in this case, had she lost the case there is the possibility her attorney could have used jurors looking at her Facebook and Linked In information as the grounds for an appeal.

Which is a good opportunity for a quick timeout. As a health care provider, be careful what you put on any profiles you post. **KEEP THEM PROFESSIONAL**. If a patient has a bad outcome and starts to look up information about you online, learning about your education and training, your years in practice, your volunteer or charity work, any areas of specialization, all of this is appropriate, especially on your practice web site. Where I cringe is when I read about someone who is married, has three "perfect" children, has a house at the beach and one in the mountains, someone who owns her own plane and enjoys flying to the family mountain retreat on weekends, or the doctor who enjoys his extensive collection of Muscle Cars housed in a special garage on his 100-acre farm. These accomplishments and passions are all something to be proud of and they are well-earned, but to an injured patient or to the attorney for an injured patient, it is the equivalent of a wounded dolphin in the middle of a school of sharks, and to a jury it might be enough to sway their opinion.

.

When the jury has reached a verdict the attorneys and their clients will be seated, the jury will return, and then the judge will enter the courtroom. The judge will ask the jury if it has reached a verdict, the jury foreman will answer "yes" if in fact it has, and the verdict will be read aloud. As you can imagine, regardless of the strength of your beliefs throughout the claim process (and if you did not believe you were not negligent you would not be standing where you are now), the strength of your fact and expert witnesses, and the quality work done by your legal team, standing with your attorney or attorneys as the verdict is about to be read is usually the most stressful time of the case, even for your attorney (their reputation is on the line, too).

Depending on the jury instructions the jury will render a verdict on whether you were negligent or not and, if you were negligent, did it result in the harm suffered by the patient. Then, depending on various factors including the state and its process, the jury will have already determined damages, if it found you to be negligent, **or** it may be asked to determine damages after the verdict has been decided. Once the verdict is read the judge will often poll the jurors quickly to make sure there is no dissent, and then the losing side will ask the court for various motions, including the court imposing a different ruling than that determined by the jury. I have only heard of one case in 25 years where the judge essentially said to the jury that he was not sure it was paying attention, but he was reversing their verdict and this reversal was, as you might imagine, immediately appealed.

The aftermath

As noted previously, one of the toughest parts about a health care provider dealing with a malpractice claim is that it is never a "one and done" situation. **First** you have the event, which as noted you may already know is going to result in a malpractice claim and, therefore, you are in a slightly hyper-vigilant state waiting for the claim to be filed. **Second** you have to deal with the claim and the claim process and (maybe) a jury trial, again very stressful. But after that you are done, right? Your life can begin returning to normal, correct? Unfortunately, not.

Third, there may an appeal regardless of the verdict. In most states, there are short, rigid time frames for filing an appeal. Unless the side filing the appeal has some sort of really, strong argument, the court will most likely reject the appeal. Then the side upset with the loss has the option of filing an appeal with either an Appeals Court or the state Supreme Court. Usually the defense (you) is more likely to do this if it believes an error of law has been made, and that is a crucial thing to remember whenever there is an appeal: <u>an appeal must turn on an issue of law, not on an issue of fact</u>. In the one case I am familiar with , the losing side tried to file an appeal with the court and in the appeal released 184 pages of "evidence" that it had not previously disclosed. What should have happened at that point is that the defendants and their attorneys should have been sanctioned for withholding evidence, which can be both a civil and criminal act, depending on the state, but in this case the defense attorneys were with Big Dawg firms so the court just ignored everything and denied the appeal.

If there is an appeal to the state Supreme Court you must prepare for a wait. All states have a time limit in which the side wishing to file a supreme court challenge can do so, but in some cases it can be as long as six months before it is filed. Then the side not filing the challenge gets to see the argument of the side appealing the verdict and it responds. While there is often a lengthy delay before the state Supreme Court rules, the good news is that any change in the verdict must ride on some rule of law, not of fact. The only other thing that can be appealed is the size of an award, but lawyers are often reluctant to appeal on this issue as "winning" the appeal usually means re-trying the case, which can result in an even greater jury verdict. The good news is that courts rarely overturn jury verdicts as it is understood the jury has rendered its verdict, based on the facts of the case, on who was right and who was wrong, which is why only issues of law can be appealed. Based on this most health care malpractice cases are not appealed.

And so now you are done, correct? No, not yet.

Fourth, depending on the state where you practice there may be a mandated report to the specialty board under whose regulations you practice, the Board of Medicine, the Board of Dentistry, the Board of Nursing, etc. If you have had a paid claim, either settlement or jury verdict, it is a given that there will be a Board review. In most cases the Board will send you a letter stating that it is aware of the claim and/or payment and would like an explanation from you. DO NOT ANSWER THIS ON YOUR OWN! The attorney who worked with you on the case should work with you on crafting an answer. In some areas, there are attorneys and law firms that specialize in this work and you may end up working with them. Their role is to keep you from making a bad situation worse by saying something in your response that draws the attention of the Board and results in a deeper investigation of you, your practice, even of your partners.

Hopefully the Board accepts your response without taking further action but if it does decide to open a deeper investigation this will, again, ratchet up all your stress responses. As this investigation could result in further action against you, an attorney should guide you through this process as well; the only question will be if your professional liability company will pay for this or if you must pay out of your own pocket.

At about the same time, if you are a physician and if any payment has been made you will also be reported to the National Practitioner Data Bank ("NPDB"), a federal registry intended to help stop "bad" physicians from crossing state lines to continue practicing. Most of the report is cut-and-dried facts, but there will be a summary of the allegations included and at the very end you are given a brief opportunity to present your side of the story. However, this process once again brings the entire episode back to life in your mind and elevates your stress level again.

But once this is done you are finished with this claim, correct? **NO.** Depending on circumstances in the near and distant future you should or may have to:

- Deal with an increase in your malpractice premiums. At the very least if you were receiving a claim-free or loss-free credit that credit will be removed for a period and then will rebuild slowly over a period of years, reducing your income.
- Depending on the location of your practice and the amount of media coverage, you may have to

.

deal with rebuilding your reputation; reduce stress by developing, with professional help if necessary, a "spin phrase" or series of safe phrases to address any patient or media questions, phrases that don't invite further litigation but also paint you in the best light. Preparing these phrases ahead of time means you are taking control of the situation, reducing your distress. In addition, and trust me on this, someone asking you to talk about it is better than an awkward silence as you cannot interpret their silence.

- In addition to the loss of any claim-free or loss-free credits, if a paid claim is large enough the insurance company may choose to debit your account, so you lose a credit and have extra money added on to your premium. The combined impact of this can be staggering, resulting in your malpractice insurance premium doubling or more and while you're dealing with this, what surfaces at the same time? You start reliving the claim again, all the events, and if you settled you start second-guessing if settling was the right thing to do. Once again, your stress levels rise to distress levels.
- You will now have to list this claim and all the facts on every application you complete, be it for malpractice insurance, hospital credentialing, or payer credentialing. Once again you must relive the event, but here I have a recommendation for you: have the attorney who defended you write a letter describing the events, the care, the outcome, the allegation, what was paid if

.

anything, and why. By having this letter in your file to use, the claim portion of the application can simply read "See Attached" and this can greatly reduce your stress levels because you are taking control of the situation beforehand. Why not a letter from you? It is assumed that anything you write will be biased; it is assumed that anything the attorney writes will be biased, too, but much less so as the attorney has his/her own reputation to consider.

Finally, any time you must treat a patient with a complaint like the one that resulted in the claim, your stress levels will likely elevate for a while. Remember what you learned from the experience, focus on your breathing for a moment (more on that when we get to neuromuscular relaxation), and then focus on this patient and only this patient, listen, think, ask questions, be what you are: an educated, trained, experienced health care professional who is great at what you do.

4. Post-Traumatic Stress Disorder

When I first began researching this topic in 1991, the term or diagnosis of Post-Traumatic Stress Disorder ("PTSD") was not well known outside of the military world, although symptoms of trauma-related mental disorders have been documented since at least the time of ancient Greece. During the first and second World Wars, studies increased and what we today refer to as PTSD was known under various terms including "shell shock" and "combat neurosis." The term "post-traumatic stress disorder" came into use in the 1970s in large part due to the diagnoses of U.S. military veterans returning from the Vietnam War. It was officially recognized by the American Psychiatric Association ("APA") in 1980, in the third edition of the Diagnostic and Statistical Manual of Mental Disorders (DSM-III).

In the United States it is estimated that about 3.5% of adults have PTSD in any given year, and 9% of people develop it at some point in their life. In much of the rest of the world, rates during a given year are between 0.5% and 1%. Higher rates may occur in regions of armed conflict. It is more common in women than men. What is significant about this is that ongoing advances in medical technology have shown that PTSD is not just "in your head" but can cause physiological changes to the brain and how it functions. Can't find the words to express your thoughts? That's because the prefrontal lobe, responsible for language, is adversely affected by trauma. Can't regulate your emotions? The amygdala, which regulates

.

emotions, is pushed into overdrive and in some PTSD survivors the amygdala increases in size, making it more difficult to control emotion. When the amygdala revs up, "safe" situations can be perceived as unsafe, keeping someone with PTSD is a permanently aroused emotional state. Short-term memory loss? Studies show that in some PTSD survivors the hippocampus, responsible for memory and experience assimilation, shrinks. Feeling anxious and afraid? After trauma the medial prefrontal cortex, which regulates emotions, does not regulate itself after trauma. The "fight or flight" mechanism is primarily controlled by three hormones, cortisol, epinephrine, and norepinephrine. In people with PTSD cortisol production is suppressed while epinephrine and norepinephrine levels are higher than normal. Therefore, people who have suffered trauma cannot "just get over it."

PTSD, its impact and recovery, will differ from person-to-person. PTSD is defined as a condition of persistent mental and emotional stress occurring because of injury or severe psychological shock, typically involving disturbance of sleep and constant vivid recall of the experience, with dulled responses to others and to the outside world. In the immediate aftermath of a trauma, say during the first month, many people suffer from acute stress which can include the following symptoms:

- Anxiety
- Behavioral disturbances
- Dissociation
- Hyperarousal
- Avoidance of memories related to the trauma
- Flashbacks

148

.

- Nightmares

All of the above symptoms are considered normal in the days and weeks after a trauma as the survivor processes the recent event. However if the symptoms persist for more than one month, and begin to socially and functionally impair the survivor of the trauma, the diagnosis is changed to PTSD.

People diagnosed using either a military or civilian measurement tool are considered to have PTSD if they suffer from at least three of the following symptoms:

- At least one re-experiencing symptom
- At least one avoidance symptom
- At least two arousal and reactivity symptoms
- At least two cognition and mood symptoms

Re-experiencing symptoms include:

- Flashbacks—reliving the trauma over and over, including physical symptoms like a racing heart or sweating
- Bad dreams
- Frightening thoughts

Re-experiencing symptoms may cause problems in your everyday routine. The symptoms can start from your own thoughts and feelings. Words, objects, or situations that are reminders of the event can also trigger re-experiencing symptoms. For you, think closely about these last few sentences: every day you are likely to experience thoughts, feelings, and situations that result in re-experiencing symptoms simply as you practice each day.

- Staying away from places, events, or objects that are reminders of the traumatic experience
- Avoiding thoughts or feelings related to the traumatic event

Things that remind you of the traumatic event can trigger avoidance symptoms. These symptoms may cause you to change your personal routine. For example, after a bad car accident, a person who usually drives may avoid driving or <u>riding</u> in a car. You may try to avoid seeing certain types of patients who remind you of the patient who sued you for malpractice. But realistically you cannot avoid places and events or objects that remind you of the traumatic event, absent changing professions or retiring.

- Being easily startled
- Feeling tense or "on edge"
- Having difficulty sleeping
- Having angry outbursts

Arousal symptoms are usually constant, instead of being triggered by things that remind you of the traumatic events. These symptoms can make you feel stressed and angry. They may make it hard to do daily tasks, such as sleeping, eating, or concentrating. These responses are typically not readily apparent issues that are always present, but issues that arise in response to certain stimulation.

- Trouble remembering key features of the traumatic event
- Negative thoughts about yourself or the world
- Distorted feelings like guilt or blame
- Loss of interest in enjoyable activities

Cognition and mood symptoms can begin or worsen after the traumatic event. These symptoms can make you feel alienated or detached from friends or family members, something commonly described by both health care providers suffering from litigation stress and the people around them. Some people describe it as living "in someone else's skin."

It is natural to have some of these symptoms after a dangerous, threatening or traumatic event. Sometimes people have very serious symptoms that go away after a few weeks. This is called **acute stress disorder**, or ASD. When the symptoms last more than a month, seriously affect your ability to function, and are not due to substance use, medical illness, or anything except the event itself, they might be PTSD. Some people with PTSD don't show any symptoms for weeks or months. PTSD is often accompanied by depression, substance abuse, or one or more of the other anxiety disorders.

Anyone can develop PTSD at any age. This includes war veterans, children, first responders, and people who have been through a physical or sexual assault, abuse, accident, disaster, or other serious or traumatic event, or an event perceived as such including job loss and litigation. According to the National Center for PTSD, about 7 or 8 out of every 100 people will experience PTSD at some point in their lives. Women are more likely to develop PTSD than men, and genes may make some people more likely to develop PTSD than others.

Why do some people develop PTSD and other people do not?

It is important to remember that not everyone who lives through a traumatic event develops PTSD. In fact, most people will <u>not</u> develop the disorder. Many factors play a part in whether you will develop PTSD. Some examples are listed below. *Risk factors* make a person more likely to develop PTSD. Other factors, called *resilience factors*, can help reduce the risk of the disorder.

Risk Factors and Resilience Factors for PTSD

Some factors that increase risk for PTSD include:

- Living through dangerous events and traumas
- Getting hurt or injured
- Seeing another person hurt or injured, or seeing a dead body
- Childhood trauma
- Feeling horror or <u>helplessness</u>, or <u>extreme fear</u>
- <u>Having little or no social support after the event</u>

152

- Dealing with extra stress after the event, such as loss of a loved one, pain and injury, or loss of a job or home
- Having a history of mental illness or substance abuse

Some resilience factors that may reduce the risk of PTSD include:

- Seeking out support from other people, such as friends or family
- Finding a support group after a traumatic event
- Learning to feel about one's own actions in the face of danger
- Having a positive coping strategy, a way of getting through the bad event, and learning from it
- Being able to act and respond effectively despite feeling fear

Researchers are studying the importance of these and other risk and resilience factors, including genetics and neurobiology. With more research, someday it may be possible to predict who is likely to develop PTSD and to prevent it. **One of the keys to treating PTSD is removing the person from the source of the trauma**. This is why coming home from the Middle East is the first step in helping heal PTSD in a combat veteran. Recognition is another important factor; as many combat veterans discuss, they don't see anything wrong with their feelings or behavior as everyone else who served with them feels and acts the same way!

The challenge with PTSD induced by litigation is that the litigation can drag on for many years, so while you will

153

not always be active in dealing with your litigation, the source of your trauma, it does not go away, either. In addition you are forced to deal with it off and on for several years, through the litigation process itself to credentialing, possible Board of Medicine investigations, comments and questions by patients and others, and every time you apply or re-apply for malpractice insurance or credentialing. So, it takes quite some time to truly get away from the source of the trauma in the beginning, then it rears its ugly head off and on for many years into the future. The concern with this long-term exposure to the trauma is that studies have now shown conclusively, using imaging studies of the brain, that long-term exposure to PTSD results in actual physical changes to the brain. This has now been defined as "Complex-PTSD."

The first requirement for a diagnosis of Complex-PTSD is a prolonged exposure to the source of the trauma. The symptoms can include:

- Alterations in emotional regulation, such as persistent sadness, suicidal thoughts, explosive anger, or inhibited anger
- Alterations in consciousness, which can manifest as either forgetting traumatic events completely or continually reliving them, along with feeling detached from your own mental processes or body
- Changes in self-perception, which can include feelings of helplessness, shame, guilt, and a sense of being completely different than other humans

.

- Alterations in the perception of the perpetrator, including ceding total power to the perpetrator or becoming preoccupied with the relationship to the perpetrator, including a preoccupation with revenge
- Alterations in relations with others, to include personal relations, isolation, distrust, or a repeated search for a rescuer
- Changes in one's system of meanings, including a loss of faith, or a sense of hopelessness or despair

In the months immediately following a traumatic event these feelings are normal and considered to be acute stress, but if these symptoms persist for more than a few months and the above symptoms begin to be appreciated, the diagnosis changes to PTSD according the DSM-IV.

As you can see, failing to adequately deal with litigation stress, or any severe trauma, can lead to PTSD. Failure to adequately deal with PTSD can have serious, long-term consequences.

But if does not have to be this way!

5. REVIEW

What I have attempted to do up to this point is educate you about what a stress response is, how it can be divided into good stress ("eustress") and bad stress ("distress"), in some cases depending on the source of stress, the "stressor," but in most cases today it is not the event as much as it is our reaction to it. What is significant to something becoming distress, too, is not merely the severity of the event but our ability to **control** the situation; the more we can control any situation the less distress we will have, while the less control we have, or even the perception of lack of control, the more distressful something can become.

What today we call stress is actually just responding to the world around us and whether something is eustress (your child or you achieving a well-deserved award or the pre-performance jitters you experience before giving a speech or presentation to a large audience for the first time) or distress (a vehicle suddenly cutting you off in traffic, the death of someone close or a divorce, your own or someone else's) the physiological response is the same, the "fight or flight" mechanism hardwired in our DNA for thousands of years kicking in. The challenge today is that in most cases the stressor that results in distress is usually something we cannot flee or fight, cannot run away from or kill, usually the only two choices our prehistoric ancestors had when faced with a stressor causing distress, say a sabre tooth tiger. Yet even though our bodies gear up to fight or run away, gear up for action just as happened thousands of years ago, today we usually cannot fight or run away. This leaves us stewing in the juices produced by this response, the jolt of adrenaline, fats and sugars dumped into our bloodstream for energy, cortisol coursing through our arteries and veins, the increased blood flow to skeletal muscles and the decreased blood flow to internal organs, the increase in heart rate and breathing, the increased alertness, the being "on edge." This is "witches brew" occurring inside of your body every time you have a stress response, the gas pedal and brake pedal pushed all the way to the floor; the challenge is if you control it or it controls you.

After looking at stress and separating it into distress and eustress, looking at what Hans Selye called the General Adaption Syndrome, we looked at what malpractice is supposed to be legally and some things you can do to decrease the chances of a malpractice claim occurring, commonly called risk management and/or loss control. Remember that the only way to absolutely guarantee that you will never have a malpractice claim is to quit: this is called loss avoidance. You choose not to undertake the risk. Let's eliminate that as an option for now.

The items viewed in the section on how malpractice claims occur and things you can do to reduce the chance of a claim occurring you have likely heard or read before. But one forgotten part of a good risk management program is repetition: hear it and forget it, do it and remember it. But if doing something routinely is not a realistic option, the more frequently you hear it the more likely you are to retain the information. Thus, the required annual staff education in hospitals and similar facilities, and thus so very often the first word a child learns is "NO!" Repetition.

But a key point of emphasis in the section on how malpractice claims originate is the concept that while a poor outcome is usually the trigger for a malpractice claim, a poor outcome does not automatically mean malpractice, or negligence, occurred. This moved us into the next chapter on the legal process and how a malpractice claim, or any litigation, moves through the court system.

The big take-aways from the section on the legal process would include:

- Litigation is often a long process, but not continuous; you will have periods with bursts of activity followed by long periods where it appears not much, if anything, is going on. This lack of outright control puts a lot of emphasis on litigation stress management.
- Litigation is adversarial due to the process, the civil legal system today, and the training of attorneys. There are forms of Alternative Dispute Resolution, usually preferable to a jury trial, but both sides must agree to use it and using it usually means that a settlement is expected to occur.
- The civil legal system is uniformly not uniform and a malpractice case, if it gets into litigation, is usually not fair to either side: if the patient wins at trial it may make the patient more financially whole, but it will be long after the injury occurred; if you win it means a jury has found your care to not be negligent, but only after a long, challenging

.

process and the patient, likely injured, is left uncompensated but still injured.

- Once a claim moves into litigation it becomes the attorney's litigation, not your litigation, and while this is due to the process, and the training and experience of the attorney, it will tend to leave you feeling like a prop in a play, despite the best efforts of the attorney to keep you informed and involved. To you it is your reputation on the line, to the attorney it is his/her reputation on the line.
- If your case gets to a jury trial the trial itself will be a condensed version of the process, with periods of inactivity and then bursts of activity. Your ability to remain calm and focused during a trial, to keep distress at a minimum, is important to your ability to pay attention, focus, and assist your attorney.
- The most important part of any litigation is often the deposition, which is supposed to be used to learn facts about the case but is often misused by attorneys today to badger a witness into blurting out possibly damaging things or displaying behavior that you will likely be a bad witness on your own behalf. Your defense team should prepare you for the deposition, both what they will be asking you and what the opposing counsel should ask you. Stress control techniques may prove crucial during a deposition to prevent opposing counsel from getting under your skin, getting you agitated, and presenting a biased opinion of you to a jury.

159

Once you get past the hurdle of a patient with a bad outcome filing a claim against you, much of the litigation process being outside of your control becomes the primary source of litigation stress. The stress management techniques in the next chapter will prove very important in helping you keep your distress under control. But one key part of feeling some control during the litigation process is knowing the process in your jurisdiction, understanding it, knowing what to expect and when to expect it, and being emotionally, physically, and intellectually prepared to handle the ebb and flow of litigation.

Finally, we looked at Post-Traumatic Stress Disorder ("PTSD"). Over time this has come to be recognized as a very real potential consequence of any severe trauma, based on the event itself and the hardiness or resilience of the person suffering the traumatic event. The event may be physical, such as that suffered by military and first-responders, or purely emotional, such as the death of a loved one, divorce, job loss, or dealing with a malpractice claim or any form of litigation.

PTSD not only results in emotional and behavioral changes, but if allowed to persist long enough it can result in physical changes to the brain itself, essentially setting the "control panel" in the brain to become sensitized to hypervigilance, keeping your "fight or flight" response on low-level arousal continuously and making it more likely to kick into a high-level response at the slightest provocation. This can have deleterious effects on your body over the long-term, as well as impacting your behavior, your relationships, and your practice. It has even been hypothesized that after all this country has been through in

160

.

the last 20 – 30 years, the hyper-partisanship in politics, the events of 09/11/2001, two wars, the rapid rate of change brought about by the growth in technology and connectivity (both good and bad), the global economic meltdown caused by Wall Street with the resultant massive job losses and homes lost, and the Internet of Things, it has been hypothesized the country has a large number people of people, perhaps most of the citizens of this country, suffering from constant, low-level PTSD. Essentially, the argument goes, we have an entire country waiting for "what's next?" What will the next adverse event be? The result is that the "fight or flight" mechanism is always on, people are in a constant low-level state of PTSD with all the behavioral and physical challenges that come with it. And, most are not even aware of it!

·

6. Stress Management Techniques

If you can fill the unforgiving minute with sixty
seconds' worth of distance run...

In Rudyard Kipling's poem "*If*" his imagery is profound. Kipling leaves the details to us but declares what it is someone can use to measure manhood (in his day, personhood or humanity today). We understand the analogy, but the important point is what we do with the next sixty seconds. And the next sixty seconds. And then the next sixty seconds. In this section I want to impart techniques to you that make the next "unforgiving minute" something of value instead. **Going back to that one thing I asked you to remember: peace is a choice and you can choose peace right now**. This chapter is to your peace, to make the next sixty seconds worthwhile.

Mindfulness

Before delving into this chapter in too much depth I want to discuss the concept of "mindfulness." The reason is that much of what we will be talking about in this chapter is designed to lead to or promote mindfulness, which sounds as if it is something New Age but, under different names, has been around for thousands of years. But from Buddhism and ancient Greek philosophy to an app on your smart phone today, mindfulness has been a way of reducing stress. It has been further defined as an open, accepting attention to and awareness of internal and external sensations.

.

One of the biggest challenges when dealing with litigation stress, as has been noted, is the lack of control you have over the process once it is started, Lack of control creates distress and soon you can find yourself in an endless loop of thinking about the litigation, increasing your distress, and knowing where the distress is coming from results in you thinking **more** about the litigation. Consequently, you end with people, usually a significant other, asking "***Where are you?***" as you are sitting at home, in a restaurant, in church, or wherever. During my foray into litigation my wife asked me this question often. Your body is there, you are physically present, but mentally and emotionally you are miles away, thinking about the litigation or some aspect of the care rendered. Some people refer to being present as being "emotionally available."

Mindfulness strives to attain a few goals, but achieving those goals involves calming the mind's constant thought processes. As will be noted below, being aware of and sensitive to your thoughts, and the stress and distress they can arouse, can be dealt with in a variety of methods, from meditation to yoga, exercise to progressive relaxation. The surge in the concept of mindfulness today is a result of it being recognized that many people are at a certain level of "fight or flight" daily, and this has the result, as we have mentioned, of creating various deleterious effects on the body as it gears up to fight or flee, but can do neither.

An interesting way of looking at mindfulness, of gaining control of your mind, and you will find this to be true if you practice any or some of the approaches below, is that each time you work on mindfulness you are really working on not reacting. The result is that any stress response that does occur may be dampened by mindfulness or recognized and short-circuited. This has the impact of gradually reducing the flow of harmful chemicals that eat us up when we are suffering distress.

As there has been a surge in research over the last 30 years or so geared towards understanding how mindfulness positively can impact our mental, emotional, and physical health, there are a plethora of resources available on this subject, print, online, and likely some local classes of one method or another. The key is to find what works for you, what you will enjoy doing, what you will continue to do after any formal training or class work is completed. This is really training for your life and training as though your life depends on it, because it is and it does.

However, as I am fond of mentioning in my classes, all that you do will be because you want to do these things for your own good and the good of those around you, the "commitment" part of the "Three C's" (below). If you take the approach that these are things you should do but don't really want to, you end up with more stress as you are constantly telling yourself "*I should do this and I should do that*!" and you end up "shoulding" all over yourself.

Whether I am teaching a basic stress management class or dealing specifically with something such as litigation stress, there are fundamentals that apply for all stress management techniques. For example, the quicker steps are taken to reduce your distress, through education or using up the juices of stress, the better off you will be. Surgeons talk about staying in front of the "pain curve" post-surgically; similar thinking applies here.

And why might the greatest predictor of a future claim be a past claim? Taking a head-in-the-sand approach and ending up behind the stress curve; rather than dealing with your distress you try to work your way out of it. When my first marriage was ending I put in a lot of hours in the office, exactly the wrong approach! I have given you some tools to help you understand the legal event; work to separate this legal event from the medical event, understanding that the legal event is about money, but at its root it is about the desire to "get even" that is hardwired into our DNA , and the litigation process is currently the only way for the patient to "get even." This event may have been caused by the poor outcome, but is separate from the medical procedure.

Let's start with The Three C's of Coping:

1. **Commitment**: This refers to you consciously and actively involving yourself in your life, which includes efforts to get your stress to manageable levels and keeping it there. Refuse to be a victim. It may not always be easy, but peace is a choice.
2. **Control**: We have discussed this quite a bit already, but to emphasize it again most distress comes from a lack of control or a perceived lack of control, so you need to behave as though you have some influence over the course of events. Mindfulness. Victims of chronic distress often relate feeling out of control or, as the author Isaac Asimov said, "*Things are in the saddle and riding mankind.*" If this book can be reduced to one

.

sentence, one goal, it would be to help you control that which you can and deal with that which you cannot control…and if that sounds strangely like The Serenity Prayer, it is no accident.

3. **Challenge**: Change is normal and the rate of change has accelerated. Dealing with litigation will change you. Can you accept the challenge of dealing with this change and using it as a vehicle towards personal growth? In other words, adapt or die.

When assessing the stress in your life, the stress level and what has moved from simply responding to the world around you and has become distress, some control can come from formally assessing your stress:

1. What is causing your stress?
2. Why is it affecting you?
3. How is it affecting you?
4. Why are YOU allowing this to happen?
5. What are YOU going to do about it?

Two major points before we get too much further along: **first, the better you are at handling stress before becoming involved in a malpractice claim the better you will be at handling the stress of a malpractice claim.** This is why I stated there are fundamentals central to all stress management. So, if you have never been involved in a malpractice claim…well, first of all, congratulations! But this book is also designed to help you develop good coping skills, good stress management skills in your everyday life, to give you better skills, more resilience, so that when you are forced to deal with extremely stressful situations, such as a malpractice claim, you are already prepared.

Second, establish a relationship with a primary care physician if you don't already have one. One reason to do this is to establish a baseline for your health status. Another reason is that I am going to mention exercise quite frequently, to use up the "juices" of stress, and you want to know what level of exercise you can safely start at. A third reason is sleep: science is constantly discovering all of the things that occur during sleep and the bad things that can happen from lack of sleep, including an increased risk of dementia and schizophrenia. Many health care providers report sleep problems when dealing with litigation stress. You may benefit from either a sleep medication or anti-anxiety pill to help you get sufficient sleep during the course of your litigation; that is not a sign of weakness, it is a sign of awareness! But do not self-medicate!

Commitment

What is causing your stress?

Many times this can be hard to pinpoint, either because you don't know exactly where it is coming from or you are afraid to really assess the situation. In the case of dealing with a malpractice claim it is easy to pinpoint the main source of stress, but there will also be secondary sources of stress such as asking yourself if you really were negligent, if so did you harm the patient, was there something you could have done differently, with all of this possibly leading to questioning your ability as a health

167

care provider. You may bemoan your decision to take call that night so a colleague could attend his child's third grade class performance of "Our Town" by Thornton Wilder. This is an example of what is meant when experts refer to most people being able to deal with the normal stress of daily living, but begin to struggle if things build up: some people call dealing with this stress buildup being like peeling off the layers of an onion, one layer at a time, until the stress becomes small enough to be managed again, while others just refer to it as "one damn thing after another."

At its core the source of your distress is the malpractice claim and any resulting litigation, but there are sub-layers to the distress that need to be addressed. As you address these layers you gradually assume more control over the situation and the distress becomes more manageable. The major source of your distress, the malpractice claim, can loom large, but as you dispose of the sub-layers the major distress becomes more manageable. How do you eat an elephant? One bite at a time.

However, don't think that these thoughts will pop into your head automatically nor at the same time. It is likely these thoughts will show up over time, indeed often at strange times, as you sit dwelling on the major source of distress, the malpractice claim, or while you are not thinking of anything at all related to the claim. Find ways to dispose of them one at a time, from counseling to a support group (where your feelings and thoughts will be discussed, but not the specific facts of the claim, right?). Establishing a relationship with a psychologist or Licensed

Clinical Social Worker or the like, will likely be very beneficial and these conversations are privileged.

Why is it affecting you?
This is not a superficial question. Your initial reaction may be one of incredulity: "*I am being sued for malpractice, stupid!*" But the question really goes to something deeper because people get sued a lot in the United States and no one dies from litigation, making the "fight or flight" response inappropriate to some extent. So why is this affecting you?

- Is it because of a fear of losing your reputation, of embarrassing your family or facing your colleagues? Loss of reputation is horrible to deal with and I will touch more on how to deal with this in a bit.
- Does it go back to some of the issues above regarding what is causing your stress, doubts over your ability, questions about your care, an in-your-head debate over your career choice?
- Is it a fear of losing your practice, your license, your ability to earn a living?
- Is it simply the thought that you may have caused harm?

Why is this affecting you? Over time these and other issues will surface and you will face them, work through them, find the answers, and move on. They will, one by one, be addressed and cast aside. You may find the answers yourself, they may come from peers or a support group or counseling, or they may come from your defense

169

team. One thing that will help you through this part of the process goes back to something I brought up earlier in the book: "MDiety Syndrome."

As you work your way through the various issues of why this is affecting you, remember that you are a human being. Human beings make mistakes. Human beings make mistakes all the time, every day. Be gentle with yourself and go gentle on yourself. Don't beat yourself up because you were not perfect; you never were, thus you have this malpractice claim. Just be human.

How is it affecting you?

This is where we really start to dig into some coping skills that are not designed to help you control the source of your distress or your perception of control, but to help you deal with the effects of distress on you. Not your body or your mind, your mind/body. This is where we deal with the "juices" eating you up inside, the gas pedal and brake pedal stuck to the floor, the fight or flight mechanism at work when you cannot fight or run away.

One key concept to keep in mind here is the same advice you tend to give or get when dealing with that incurable illness, the common cold: there is no cure so focus on treating the symptoms. As noted, if you become involved in litigation it is a slow, uneven process; until you can remove the source of the distress, treat the symptoms.

Control

Previously we discussed control and gaining some feeling of it by educating yourself on how a malpractice case plays out in your authority. I can't emphasize enough gaining as much knowledge as you can about the whole process. The attorney assigned to defend you by your insurance company, along with the claims manager from the insurance company, are there to work for you; if you don't know what it is they are supposed to be doing you will be a passive passenger on this journey and that will not help your stress or the defense of your claim. You have more knowledge about this case than anyone: use it! Combine your knowledge of the patient and treatment and everything that happened, along with your documentation, and combine it with the litigation process to make **you** your best, strongest advocate.

This is especially true when it comes to expert witnesses. Your expert or experts can help educate your defense team on the basics, based on the facts; you, on the other hand, can educate your team and even your expert witness on the specifics of this case, this patient, and make everyone better prepared for the deposition and, if necessary, testimony of the plaintiff's expert. You are likely the only person who knows the whole story. Active participation in your own defense gives you a feeling of some control over events, helping to reduce your stress.

Challenge

Are you prepared to take on the challenge of working towards peace and wellness, of getting your stress down to a manageable level, of working on mindfulness? A reminder, before getting too far into this section: GET A PHYSICIAN! If you do not have a relationship with a physician, a primary care physician, establish one now and get a physical examination.

Lifestyle and Personality

First in this category is your **social network** and this is often where women outdistance men. Few men maintain strong social networks after entering the work world, with work and family taking up most of their focus. Go back to my comments on **loyalty.** Men tend to either have very superficial social networks (the once a week tennis foursome) or no social network outside of work. But a social network inside of work can be dangerous during a malpractice claim as discussion of the claim is hard to avoid. Always rely on the advice of your attorney, but one key admonition is to not discuss the facts of the case except under the privilege afforded by the attorney-client relationship.

However, discussing your feelings, discussing your fears, hopes, how you are holding up is acceptable and may speak to counseling or a support group. The challenge is that just when you want to talk about this patient and the treatment the most, you should say the least. Blame it on your attorney or blame it on the insurance company, realistically blame it on the legal system we have, say in a lighthearted manner *"I'd love to discuss this in more detail but my attorney/insurance company will kill me if I do"* and move on to *"Hey! The Cubs finally won the World Series, too bad I am a White Sox fan."* Which describes me, by the way.

But the other aspect of a good social network is an emphasis on the word "social." Hopefully you can develop a group, if you don't have one already, where you can talk about anything but work, thus talk about anything but the claim. And why wait until you have a claim already? Multiple studies have shown that strong social support groups reduce stress and add to longevity, it's likely one reason married men live longer than single men. Start working on developing a social support network outside of work **now**.

Is this important? Yes. Clarity on this came to me many years ago from a television show called *"Evening Shade,"* starring Burt Reynolds as a former professional football player who returns to his home town of Evening Shade, Arkansas. Playing the local doctor, Harlan Elldridge, M.D., was the actor Charles Durning. Durning's character had a younger wife, played by Ann Wedgeworth, and one episode was devoted to the Durning character retiring. Or trying to. As he tried to slip into retirement he started driving everyone around him crazy. At the end of the show he admitted that it seemed he had always been a doctor and that he did not know what or who he was when he was not a doctor. This describes many doctors I have spoken to and worked with over the years.

I touched on this earlier: being a doctor is what you do, not WHO you are. I have worked with dozens of doctors who have retired, only to un-retire six months to a year later because they did not know what to do when not being a doctor. Start NOW, before a malpractice claim if you have not had one, before retirement is looming, to begin focusing on WHO you are and developing a life focused around WHO you are, not what you do. Doing so now reduces your stress now, can help you if you decide to retire, and will pay big dividends in separating what you do from who you are if you are ever named in a malpractice suit, helping to reduce your distress.

Ability to use time

Time is all we have. Trite, but true. We read a lot today about work-life balance. Historically doctors have tended towards workaholism. Younger physicians have been said to be uninterested in independent practice because they are not willing to put in the 60-hour weeks necessary to build and maintain such a practice. Dentists, on the other hand, seem to learn early on that if they work five-day weeks the patients seen on day five are not getting the same quality of care as those seen on day one, dentistry being more physical. I would argue that if a practice has a good administrator, or a good office manager with good consultant support, a work-life balance can be maintained in an independent practice. And you'll be a lot happier than if you are owned by a hospital or a Wall Street firm, as is in vogue as I write this. You spent years in education and training, and likely a lot of money, to learn how to do what you do, so why should you be told what to do by someone who does not know what you do? Is it, today, all about money and nothing else?

And this is true before a malpractice claim arises; it becomes more important if a malpractice claim arises. Just as people who are recently separated and/or going through a divorce tend to bury themselves in work, as it takes their minds off the marital woes and allows them to focus on something over which they have some control, you are likely to bury yourself in work if you have a malpractice claim. **Don't.** All it will do is increase the chances of burnout and likely end up increasing other

174

stress levels to distress levels. Physical resilience is critical when dealing with litigation; **litigation is a marathon, not a sprint**. By engaging in activities that even out your life between work and everything else, activities that help separate who you are from what you do, you will be more in control of both your personal and professional lives.

Attitudes

Several times throughout this work I have mentioned, directly or indirectly, attitude, peace, choices. Look at it this way: all professions have people who get sued, lawyers, accountants, insurance agents, architects; why does litigation stress hit health care providers so hard? Well, we have looked at the reasons why and they are legitimate, but that still does not prevent you from changing...or trying to change...your attitude about the event. The more dispassionate you can remain, the less susceptible you are to litigation stress. Other professionals see litigation as just a part of doing business in America today, but their litigation usually does not involve a physically injured plaintiff at the other end.

What can help is compartmentalizing events and actions. There is your practice, where you have treated hundreds, likely thousands of patients without incident; then there is one patient who believes he/she has been harmed by you, they believe they are entitled to compensation for their injuries, and just about the only way to get it is through litigation. In other words, this is about money, there is a process that everyone must go through to get it, but this is separate from who you are and the many successful outcomes you have achieved.

.

Sounds simple, doesn't it? As I sit here writing it sounds simple to me, too. But I know from experience that in reality it is quite challenging, but possible. Changes in attitudes.

Religion

I understand that this subject can be a touchy topic today as the world grows smaller due to communication devices and the internet, and the 24X7 cable news cycle. If we are going to worship a god or a God, who should we worship, which religion is the one best religion? Are they all the same? Is religion just an opiate for the masses? Is it OK to be spiritual rather than religious?

It doesn't matter. What matters is what you believe in and that may or may not include organized, formal religion. Among the core of most religions is one thought:

When life is too much to stand, try kneeling.

That quote came off a wood carving I saw at a Lowe's store! I am sure it can be traced back to something deep, but I just happened to have my eyes open today and I saw it. Keep your eyes open and look around you, always. Soak it all in, don't miss anything!

But the above little saying is true. Whether you believe in prayer as a form of salvation, a request for help, a way to give thanks, or believe it is simply a form of meditation, there is certainly nothing wrong with asking for help from above if the weight of litigation stress becomes too much. Nor is there anything wrong with talking to a

176

religious person about the emotions you are dealing with, how there are days you feel as if you are reliving the story of Job. The irony of the story of Job from the Bible is that is has led people to try and understand why bad things happen to good people; after the last 30 years or so in the U.S. I am more interested in learning why good things happen to bad people.

Is this litigation worth giving your life for?
Telomeres. Ever hear of them? No, this is not a Jimmy Buffett song. There are a lot of things you can do to deal with stress, use up the symptoms of stress, develop resilience to stress. But you can benefit your body more than 30 trillion ways with a little effort.

Your body has about 30 trillion cells (you remember this from your cellular biology classes, right?). Each of these cells contains chromosomes and at the end of every chromosome is a telomere, a layer of extra DNA that helps cells divide. But every time a cell divides the telomere frays a little bit. This contributes to aging, heart disease, cancer and diabetes. Research indicates there are four basic steps you can take to reduce wear and tear on your telomeres. And (spoiler alert) they will help with litigation stress, too.

- Nourish your DNA. The big one that most doctors and nutritionists are talking about is omega-3 fatty acids, how we have lost them in the processed foods we eat, but how we can raise the level in our diets. By increasing these anti-inflammatory fatty acids we shield our telomeres from damage. Want to create havoc on your telomeres?

177

.

Processed (farmed) red meat and sugar have a very potent negative effect on telomeres. The "old" red meat, grass fed, free-range, and organic will work better, along with fatty fish such as salmon and tuna, and avocado. In fact, as a side note, if you have never seen a piece of wild salmon (normally called "Alaskan") alongside of a piece of farm-raised salmon (normally called "Atlantic") the difference in appearance is remarkable. You will not believe they are both called salmon.

- Be positive. Much of this book is spent trying to help you separate who you are from what you do, and being able to do this will help you remain positive. Cynicism, hostility, and pessimism are hard on your telomeres. Fixating on negative thoughts pumps out stress hormones, putting you in a constant state of fight or flight even if you are not consciously aware of it. One thing recommended: *thought distancing*. Pretend your distress is being played out on a movie screen in front of you and you are just part of the audience watching it go by.
- Run away from aging. According to multiple studies, exercise is the single most important tool you can use to protect your telomeres because it busts two negative influences on your telomeres, inflammation and stress. When you likely feel like exercising the least is when exercise is most important. In one study it appeared that moderate

178

.

cardiovascular activity, something done at least three days per week for a minimum of 45 minutes, may increase production of an enzyme called telomerase that actually helps repair frayed telomeres. Warning...and this honestly does conflict with some other advice in this book...if you work out too hard, if you try to cram your workout into a "weekend warrior" type of mega-workout, overtraining may harm telomeres by messaging your body you are in a severe "flight or fight" mode.

- Re-think your vacation. Mindless lounging on a beach sounds inviting, but for telomere repair you will be better off going on a six-day meditation retreat, a "mindfulness" retreat which has been shown to stimulate telomere repair. You can do your own mindfulness retreat as a "staycation." But even if you opt for the beach it is fine if you spend time focusing on relaxation and other stress management techniques; many companies are offering additional pay for going on vacation without any electronic devices, going off the grid! If you dedicate a vacation or even a "staycation" to working on managing your litigation distress, develop skills to deal with daily stress and working on stress resilience, it will help with your litigation stress, but also may increase your life span! *Is a malpractice claim worth a shorter life?* If the answer is "no," you are on the right track with these activities.

Fitness and activity levels

I have already discussed exercise as it relates to dealing with the effects of distress on aging. Now let's discuss it purely from a stress management and fitness perspective. But first one caveat: there has been a lot of research and theories about exercise, life span, hardiness, fitness, and the like. You can find something to fit just about anyone's schedule, interest, and fitness level. The key is to find two or three things that challenge you, that you can increase as your become more fit, but that you can look at almost as play. And I mean exactly that, play.

If you look at what we did as children, assuming a fairly normal childhood, we did not do biceps curls, but we did lift things. We did not plop down on a stationary bike and pedal while watching TV. We did not run on a treadmill or cross-trainer or elliptical machine, but we did walk, jog, run and jump, up hills, over logs, around the backyard playing tag. We played and very rarely was it in a straight line. Keep that in mind. Play! Variety! Push and Pull! And stretch!

If stress is responding to the world around you and both eustress and distress gear the body up for fight or flight, why not fight or flee? Why not use up the juices of stress in exercise? The blood is flowing to your skeletal muscles gearing them up to do something, **so do something**! It can be as simple as walking, biking or swimming, or you can throw yourself into hard, grueling workouts that not only burn up the juices of stress but take your mind temporarily off the stressor. Want to fight instead? Find a gym with a heavy bag or join a martial arts studio; you can't, or shouldn't, punch out the plaintiff or the attorney, as gratifying as that may be, but you can punch something in their steed! And speaking from personal experience I will tell you that going 15 rounds of three minutes each on a heavy bag, with one minute of rest between rounds, will definitely use up the juices of stress! You may have to start with five rounds of two minutes each. And how is it that I know how grueling 15 rounds of three minutes each is with a heavy bag? Read the epilogue.

You may be thinking that this does nothing about control and does not solve the problem. <u>Correct</u>! Remember we are treating the *symptoms*. Like we treat most viruses, like we treat the common cold. Treat the symptoms. Your body wants to fight or flee, so let it! And doing so takes your mind off the litigation, if only for a little while. Control of your mind returns to you. Mindfulness.

A word of caution. Walking is a wonderful exercise, especially normal walking outside. Studies have shown that the normal motion of walking outside burns more calories than walking on a treadmill. Why? Outside you have to vary your stride length, sometimes lift your feet higher, walk uphill and downhill. What is the caution? Walking is a great exercise if you want to think! This is OK if you are thinking about things in general or working on a problem or just thinking about what you are seeing around you. Walking is **not** so great if you keep turning the claim over and over in your mind, thinking about the treatment, thinking about the deposition, thinking about the plaintiff's attorney, thinking about the treatment that resulted in the claim. If you can walk and think about anything <u>but</u> the claim, great! If you find yourself chewing on the claim the entire time you're are walking, do something else for a while.

Diet and Nutrition

Similar to exercise, if your lifestyle has resulted in some less-than-optimal diet habits, use this time to focus on you by focusing on diet and nutrition. Research local nutritionists or ask for recommendations, or go online or find a book store. You will find hundreds of books on healthy eating, many of them contradictory. One thing you can do if you have the time and money is establish a relationship with a health coach, slightly different from a life coach in that a health coach works with you on fitness and nutrition. But two simple rules I have learned over the years may be enough to get you through. **First,** eat it as it grows. I am not promoting the Paleo Diet here, but what I am saying is that the closer something is to its state in nature when you eat it, the healthier your diet will become. Your first thought may be that donuts don't grow in nature. Bingo! Your first step towards better eating. Simple, wasn't it?

Second, a fitness reporter noted that his father, who did no exercise, stayed at about the same weight year-after-year, while the reporter was a workout fanatic and having trouble controlling his weight. When he finally asked his father how he managed to keep his weight under control with the passing years, the father imparted some of the best, yet simplest, wisdom I have heard: "*When my pants start to get tight, I eat less food.*"

This is a generalization, but health care providers tend to make lousy patients, so in addition to exercise and looking at your nutrition habits, if you have not established a continuing relationship with a primary care physician now is the time to do so, as mentioned previously. Do **not**

182

self-treat. Do **not** self-medicate. Do **not** self-prescribe. If you have not been physically active you will want to check with a physician before getting started on a fitness regimen anyway, so get that annual physical you have been putting off. Change your perspective: <u>you are now in training for a marathon</u> so change your habits to those of training for a marathon; if the national occurrence-to-settlement lag time for a claim is 4.9 years, per the National Practitioner Data Bank, look at lifestyle changes in diet and exercise that prepare you for this 4.9 year marathon.

Also note that there is a great deal of information on fitness programs available today, in book stores, on the internet, on TV, and at local gyms. Also note that there is, in my mind, three types of exercise: exercise, working out, and training. The differences between each are related to intensity and duration, along with whatever **goal** you are trying to accomplish. **<u>Exercise</u>** can be walking, jogging, spending 30 minutes on an exercise bike or elliptical trainer. Just enough to keep everything in working order and eat up some of the juices of stress.

Next up would be **<u>working out</u>**. This is exercise taken to another level. When I was a regular runner I irritated the lateral meniscus on my left knee. In getting it treated the physical therapist made a comment about runners thinking that is all they need to do to stay healthy, run, ignoring strength, flexibility, the upper body, etc. He made a comment about the future containing a lot of 70-year old people with amazing cardiovascular systems who do not have the upper body strength to pick up their grandchildren. That hit home! And so I run less, if at all, but I work out hard. I use cardio to warm up and get my

183

.

heart into the what most people consider the training zone (220 minus your age, multiplied by 60% will give you a minimum, with 80% of that figure a maximum...for most people) and then use circuit weight training to keep my heart rate up while building or maintaining strength. I try to work hard for at least an hour at every work out, but I usually do not work out every day and there are days where I will simply go for a walk. There are books that state you must work out hard every day, but not the same exercises, to reduce stress and fight off aging; there are other books which state working hard every day essentially exacerbates the fight or flight mechanism by signaling the body you are fighting or fleeing every day. I am working out for life, no other goals.

So if I am working out for life am I not **training** for something? I suppose one could argue that, but to me if someone is training it is with a specific goal in mind. What is your target? To be a college football player? To be a competitive swimmer? To fight in a Mixed Martial Arts competition? To be the oldest Ninja Warrior or Cross-Fit competitor? Those would all require work outs, true, but specific work outs to achieve specific goals, training for something specific, just as you trained to take any exams you had to take in school or training. For example, people training for Mixed Martial Arts competition will frequently warm up, spar, work on specific moves, lift weights, and then finish with body weight exercises. In one case I have read of competitors finishing every training session with 250 body weight squats! Impressive? Heck yes (I have only been able to get up to 50...so far). But do you need to push that hard? Maybe you do. Maybe that is what it will take for YOU to deal with litigation stress...or even the stress of everyday life. But you don't necessarily have to go that hard, at least not every day.

This section appears short, but that is only because it is difficult to come up with a specific diet and exercise plan for someone I have never met. Let me be clear that the four most important things you can do to treat the symptoms associated with the distress caused by the stressor of a malpractice claim are education, diet, and exercise, followed by what is in the next section, relaxation skills.

Relaxation skills

Back to mindfulness!

Am I talking about meditation here? That is one possibility but it doesn't have to be that involved. If you are interested in pursuing something along this path, note that they are all trying to get you to the same place I am and you have your choice of Buddhism (meditation); Christianity (attentiveness); Hinduism (mantra); Islam (intention); or, Judaism (unplugging). You can certainly treat the symptoms by using meditation or yoga or prayer, all of which require you to focus on something other than the litigation, which is the key point. I am a proponent of something similar to meditation, but simpler: neuromuscular, or progressive, relaxation.

The thought that wasted time is time well spent comes from another boy from Illinois, Brett Eldredge. When caught up in litigation stress it is hard to think of anything else except the litigation; if you are a fan of vinyl records you know what I mean about a scratch in the record causing the verse to repeat, repeat, repeat, thus the expression "like a broken record." Your mind will be like a broken record if you let it, but be it exercise or relaxation skills, anything that takes your mind off the litigation reduces the stress. As noted, some people bury themselves in work or in constantly researching or rehashing the case, to try and take their minds off litigation stress; but, purposefully working at getting control of your mind, and thus reducing the fight or flight chemicals in your body, may seem like wasted time, but it is time well spent.

Truth be told I found neuromuscular, or progressive, relaxation by accident. I had an interest in this sort of activity (I was a health education major with a psychology minor) and needed a course such as this for graduation, and the course on neuromuscular relaxation fit my schedule. That is the only reason I took the course, it fit my schedule. It also changed my life.

The goal of neuromuscular relaxation is to greatly reduce, if not eliminate, physical stress and tension in your body by first controlling what your mind is thinking of. What started out as a challenge for me (I tend towards a Type A personality) not only became gradually easier as the semester wore on, but as I continued working on neuromuscular relaxation I progressed to the point where I was able to get my mind under control in just a few seconds, quickly check my body for stress points and let them go, and in less than one minute return to what I was doing, feeling better and refreshed.

In a live seminar, be it litigation stress or any other stress management seminar, I actively take the participants through an abbreviated session to demonstrate the basics, and then encourage them to work on what they have learned at every opportunity. I have

.

been fortunate in that some workshops participants have reported back that they have practiced and they were amazed at not only how well it worked, but at how quickly the ability to turn it on and off developed. As you and I are not live I am going to take you through an introductory session in the book, but to do so I want you to read about the process first, to understand the ending we are heading to, and then actually go through the process. See the whole thing, learn the parts, do the whole thing.

To understand one of the basic tenets of neuromuscular relaxation is to understand how we should breathe. Recall that the diaphragm separates the thoracic cavity from the abdominal cavity, creating air pressure on the lungs. The diaphragm is somewhat bell-shaped. When we inhale, the diaphragm should go down, expanding the thoracic cavity, decreasing air pressure on the lungs, and allowing the lungs to expand. As this occurs the abdominal cavity should expand slightly, what is often called "**belly breathing**." As the lungs expand we inhale. The opposite occurs when we exhale: the diaphragm moves up increasing the air pressure on our lungs, the lungs are squeezed, and we exhale. At the same time our abdominal area should contract slightly as the internal air pressure changes.

This is a normal process that can be seen very clearly when we exercise, as the body takes over and does what is correct; you cannot exercise, even at a moderate level, without belly breathing unless you force yourself not to do so. However, when we are under stress, especially excessive stress, we tend to fall into **chest breathing**, the sort of heaving that occurs in a young child when he/she is upset and sobbing: when we inhale our chest expands,

187

.

not our abdomen, and as we exhale our chest falls or contracts. This is a very inefficient way of breathing and exacerbates distress.

Thus we begin our neuromuscular relaxation class by practicing belly breathing. I want you to move to a comfortable position that you can maintain for 20-30 minutes; it can be sitting up, reclining, or lying down. If you will be lying on your back, you may want to roll up a towel or small blanket to place under your knees and/or the small of your back to take the stress off your lower back. Get comfortable!

Next I want you to place your hands on your abdomen, just rest them there. With your hands resting on your abdomen I want you to inhale and consciously push your abdomen out, hold it for a second, then allow your abdomen to relax which will cause you to exhale. This is the proper way of breathing (without forcing the abdomen out) and I want you to set a timer or alarm for five minutes and engage in this breathing activity for the next five minutes, just practicing inhale = abdomen out, exhale = abdomen in. Ignore your lungs. Inhale = abdomen out, exhale = abdomen in. Focus only on your breathing, focus only on this sensation of breathing normally over and over. If your mind begins to stray as this belly breathing becomes more second nature to you, refocus on your abdomen, out as you inhale, in as you exhale. When the alarm goes off, stop it, then take one "cleansing breath" where you inhale deeply, abdomen out, hold it for a count of five seconds, then exhale by allowing your abdomen to relax.

As you progress through this first session and each subsequent session you should notice that you are no longer consciously belly-breathing but it is happening naturally. In the beginning I asked you to consciously push your abdomen out as you inhaled, but shortly after starting, likely about the time your mind started to wander, you began breathing this way naturally. Nevertheless, I still want you to just focus on your breathing, belly breathing, feeling the air move in and out, feeling your lungs expand because you are allowing the body to work the way it was intended to.

Now I want you to think about how you feel. How do you feel after spending time not thinking about the malpractice claim or most anything else? Relaxed? Refreshed? Has the stressor, the source of your distress, been removed? **No**. But you have taken control of your mind back from the endless film loop that has been running for some time, maybe since the day of the occurrence that resulted in the malpractice suit, certainly since the malpractice suit was filed. Doing nothing more than NOT thinking about the claim has reduced your distress level, returned control of your mind to you and, most importantly, reduced the "fight-or-flight" chemicals churning up your body.

For the first week I want you to spend 20-30 minutes each day simply sitting or lying quietly and practicing your belly breathing. If you honestly don't have a 20-30 block of time to spend doing this (some doctors have told me this is not possible and my response was to think seriously about that statement and what it says about the stress of their daily lives), break it up into three sessions of 10 minutes each or two sessions of 15 minutes each or 30 sessions of one minute each! With each successive session it should become easier and easier to fall into

189

.

rhythmic belly breathing, to the point where you may find yourself unconsciously doing so during the day.

Reducing distress by removing tension
The next step in learning neuromuscular relaxation is to learn how to identify areas of tension and learn how to relax them. In doing so you may find out where you "carry" your stress or distress: do you get headaches, a stiff neck, is it sore between your shoulder blades or is your lower back tight? During the next phase you may find out where you carry your distress, if you don't already know, and learn how to reduce or eliminate the tension.

For the next phase, you might want to use a clock to help you keep track of time or even a timer to let you know when to move on. You will only need it for the first five minutes of each session. Have a partner or spousal unit? Work on this together, first one of you and then the other. What I want you to do is assume your comfortable position and begin belly breathing. By now, if you have practiced, it should only take you a couple of minutes to fall into the soft, rhythmic breathing, your mind should be easily focused on your breathing, and you should feel relaxed.

At the end of five minutes you will start identifying feelings of tension and learn how to mentally let them go. To do this you will go through the following simple routine:
1. Fan the toes out on your left foot and flex your foot up towards your knee. Hold it for about 10 seconds. Feel the tension. Experience the tension. Hold it. Now let it go. Relax your foot. Feel the loss of tension, feel the relaxed feeling in the left foot, feel the difference between tension and relaxation.

190

.

2. Return to focusing only on your breathing for about a minute.
3. Repeat the process above with your right foot.
4. Return to focusing on your breathing for about a minute.
5. Next, tighten up your left calf muscles. How you do it will be up to you: you can either flex your foot up again, flex the foot down, of just tighten the calf muscles. Hold it for about 10 seconds. Feel the tension. Experience the tension. Hold it. Now let it go. Relax your calf muscles. Let the tension go. Feel the loss of tension, feel the relaxed feeling in your calf muscle, feel the difference between tension and relaxation.
6. Return to focusing on your breathing for about a minute.
7. Repeat the process in #5 with your right calf muscles.
8. Return to focusing on your breathing for about a minute.
9. Next I want you to tighten your left upper-leg muscles, the quadriceps and hamstring muscles in your left upper leg. Normally this can be accomplished by straightening the leg and lifting it slightly, whether you are seated or standing. Tighten the muscles, hold it for about 10 seconds, feel the tension, experience the tension. Now let it go. Relax the muscles in your left upper leg. Let the tension go. Consciously feel the difference between tension and relaxation.
10. Return to focusing on your breathing for about a minute.

191

.

11. Repeat the steps in #9 with your right leg. Experience the tension, let it go, feel the difference between tension and relaxation.
12. Next, I want you to clench your buttocks and lower back muscles, tighten the muscles in your buttocks. Usually this can be accomplished by performing what is known as a pelvic tilt, rotating your hips forward, rounding the small of your back, and clenching. Hold it for about 10 seconds. Feel the tension. Experience the tension. Now let it go. Consciously relax the muscles. Feel the difference between tension and relaxation.
13. **NOW we are going to take a brief intermission**. We have, in short order, worked our way from your toes to your buttocks, alternately tensing, relaxing, experiencing, and then returning to our breathing. Now I want you to spend the next minute or so focusing solely on your breathing, then I want you run a "check" of your lower body. While still maintaining your belly breathing, consciously work your way from your toes to your buttocks checking for any signs of tension. If you find any tension, let it go. Consciously let the tension go and feel the relaxation. Before moving on I don't want you to have any tension in your lower body as we work on your upper body. So, focus on your breathing, relax, check for any tension in your lower body, let it go, focus on your breathing.
14. You will now begin working on the upper body starting with your abdominal muscles. Pull your

192

.

abdominal muscles in, hold for a count of five seconds. Next push your abdominal muscles out, hold for a count of five seconds. Finally tighten up your abdominal muscles as if someone is about to punch you in the stomach and hold this tension for about 10 seconds. Feel the tension. Experience the tension. Now relax. Consciously let the tension go. Feel the difference between tension and relaxation.

15. Return to focusing on your breathing for about the next minute.

16. Next I want you to tighten your left fist into a ball, a tight ball. Just your fist, not your forearm. Dig your finger nails into the palm of your hand and squeeze. Hold it for about 10 seconds. Feel the tension. Experience the tension. Now relax, let the tension go. Focus on the feeling of relaxation. Feel the difference between tension and relaxation.

17. Return to focusing solely on your breathing for about the next minute.

18. Now tighten your right fist into a ball, just your fist, not your forearm. Squeeze. Dig your nails into the palm of your hand. Hold it for about ten seconds. Feel the tension. Experience the tension. Now let it go. Relax. Feel the difference between tension and relaxation.

19. Return to focusing on your breathing for about the next minute.

20. Next, we'll focus on the forearm muscles by clenching your left fist into a ball, then flex your wrist back for about five seconds tensing the back

.

of your forearm. Then curl your wrist forward, tensing the front or bottom of your forearm. Hold that tension for about 10 seconds. Feel the tension. Feel the forearm grow tired. Now relax. Let the tension go. Feel the relaxation. Feel the difference between tense muscles and relaxed muscles.

21. Return to focusing on your breathing for about the next minute.

22. Next, we'll focus on your right forearm muscles by clenching your right fist into a ball, then flex your wrist back for about five seconds tensing the back of your forearm. Then curl your wrist forward, tensing the front or bottom of your forearm. Hold that tension for about 10 seconds. Feel the tension. Feel the forearm grow tired. Now relax. Let the tension go. Feel the relaxation. Feel the difference between tense muscles and relaxed muscles.

23. Focus on your breathing, only your breathing, for the next minute.

24. Now focus on your upper-left arm by straightening your arm and tensing the muscles of your triceps, the back of your arm. Hold it. Feel the tension. Hold it for about 10 seconds. Now relax. Let it go. Feel the relaxation. Focus on the difference between tension and relaxation.

25. Now focus on your breath, only on your breathing. For approximately the next minute make sure you are belly breathing, in and out, breathe naturally.

26. Next focus on your upper-right arm by straightening the arm and tensing the muscles in

.

your right triceps, the back of your arm. Tense it, hold it, feel the tension. Hold it for about 10 seconds. Now relax, let the tension go. Feel the relaxation. Feel the difference between tension and relaxation. Focus on that difference.

27. Return to focusing on your breathing for approximately the next minute.

28. Next focus on your upper-left arm again by curling your arm up and tensing your left biceps by making a muscle. You may find the entire arm is tense and that is fine. Focus on the tension for about 10 seconds, think about how it feels. Now relax, let the tension go, let your arm hang limp by your side. Feel the difference between tension and relaxation.

29. Return to focusing on your breathing for approximately the next minute.

30. Next focus on your upper-right arm by curling your arm up and tensing your right biceps by making a muscle. Your entire arm may tense and that is fine. Focus on the tension for about 10 seconds, experience it. Now let the tension go, let the arm relax. Allow the arm to hang limp by your side. Feel the difference between tension and relaxation.

31. Focus on your breathing. Focus only on your breathing for about one minute.

32. Next, we want to focus on your neck and shoulders. Hunch your shoulders up, try to draw your trapezius muscles up around your ears. Tighten your shoulders and neck, perhaps the way you do when you are under stress. Hold that

.

tension for about 10 seconds, feel it, experience it. Think about how it feels. Now relax, let it go. Let the tension run out of your fingertips. Allow the tension to leave and feel the relaxation. Experience the difference between tension and relaxation. Relax your muscles.

33. Return to focusing on your breathing for approximately the next minute.

34. Now scrunch up all the muscles in your face. You might look silly but who cares? Tighten all of your facial muscles and hold it. Feel the tension. Experience the tension. Now let it go, let the tension run down your shoulders, down your arms, and out your fingertips. Feel the relaxation, experience it. Feel the difference between tension and relaxation.

35. Return to your breathing. Focus solely on your breathing for approximately the next minute. Feel the air moving in and out through your nose. Feel your abdomen expand as you inhale and contract as you exhale.

36. Finally, it's time for one last check. Mentally assess each area of your body. Check for any area that feels tense. If you find any tension, let it go. Relax. There should be no tension anywhere in your body.

37. Focus on your breathing for about the next minute. Focus solely on your breathing.

38. Finish with a cleansing breath, one deep breath in, allow your abdomen to expand, hold it, now let it go and exhale. Relax.

.

How does an exercise such as this help? Well, how do you feel right now? Has the law suit disappeared? No. But if you did this exercise correctly, for approximately the last 30 minutes you have not thought about the suit. It has not been front and center in your mind, stirring up the juices of stress, pressing your gas pedal and brake pedal to the floor at the same time. You did not assume control over the law suit, but for the last 30 minutes or so **the law suit has not been in control over you**. You could not gain control over the source of your distress, so you treated the symptoms and gained control of your body.

Some concluding thoughts on neuromuscular, or progressive, relaxation.

- If you have a spouse or significant other, they are feeling distress also. One good way to make this activity better and more rewarding is to share it with your spouse or significant other by having them read the directions to you as you go through the exercise, freeing you up to focus on the activity itself. Then swap roles with you reading the directions and the other person going through the exercise.
- You can also record the directions and time them out as you do, which again frees you up to focus on the activity. Just make sure your voice projects calmness and not anxiety ("Relax your fist, damn it!).
- If you either have someone to share this with or elect to record your own voice, one way to make these sessions more productive, especially in the beginning, is to hold the tension for 30 seconds,

.

then relax. By holding the tension for 30 seconds, as is the case with a live seminar, you not only grow more sensitive to the feeling of tension but the muscle also more readily relaxes from fatigue, so it is easier to move from tension to relaxation.

- The more frequently you practice neuromuscular relaxation, the more proficient you will become at all aspects of it: breathing correctly, becoming more sensitive to and being able to identify stress and tension in your body, and much more proficient at releasing the tension as it begins to feel increasingly unnatural to you.

- I encourage you to find a minute or two every day where you can spend some time practicing your "belly breathing" and then quickly surveying your body for tension and letting it go. The more often you practice, even if only for minute, the better you become at performing it…which only makes sense, correct?

At this point some of you may be asking why you should not practice this every day, even if you are not involved in a malpractice claim. <u>That is a great question and the answer is mindfulness:</u> **<u>you should start practicing now</u>**! In fact, as we come down the home stretch you will see what I meant way back at the beginning, **that how you handle stress now, before you are involved in a claim or suit, will influence how well you do or do not handle litigation stress.**

There is enough stress in our lives today that practicing this relaxation technique often will not only bring you benefits on a daily basis now, but having already worked

198

on this technique will make it easier for you to control your thoughts and the juices of stress if you do become involved in a malpractice suit. Start right now!

7. Post-litigation Activities

OK, your dance with the collision between health care and the legal system is over. Most likely you have won, but if you did not I hope that you have come to some peace with it. But that brings up a good point: you have survived the rigors of a malpractice claim, now what?

In his book "*Bounce Back: Overcoming Setbacks to Succeed in Business and in Life*," University of Kentucky basketball coach John Calipari spends a lot of the book talking about bouncing back, moving on, not dwelling on the past, focusing on the future, looking forward, and putting the past behind you (this last one being something doctors are usually good at, but only when they are in control), except for one chapter. In Chapter 4 he says to break his "don't look back" rule and spend some time going back over everything that happened in explicit, excruciating detail and be brutally honest with yourself: what could you have done differently to change the outcome? Maybe something, maybe nothing. Remember, the case is over now, you can reflect on everything from the start of the patient-physician relationship through whatever it was that resulted in a malpractice claim being filed against you, how the claim went, any settlement or jury verdict, the whole thing. Don't dwell on it but take some time, an hour, a day, no more than a week to "stay under the covers" and dwell. Feel sorry if necessary. Then that is it, it is over, time to learn and move on!

The key point here is to learn as much as possible about the entire experience, including the actions and support of the people around you. This event impacted people around you, too: any fences to mend? Anyone to thank? Make a list, check it twice. REMEMBER: you are still you, something extremely emotional happened to you, you have survived it, and now you WANT to return to the you who existed before the claim, the same confident, competent, caring person you were before. This "pity party" exercise is really designed to "clear the decks" and get everything out so you can move on with purpose and passion.

Next, like it or not you are now somewhat of an expert on malpractice claims, litigation, litigation stress, from occurrence to closure. If anyone helped you, pay it forward. If no one helped you, you be the foundation on which something can be built, some sort of group talk. Nothing formal, and no discussion of the specifics of the claim unless you arrange for some sort of attorney privilege, which would be difficult in this situation, but a support group, an "I have walked in your shoes and I am here to help" group. You might even draw in some other doctors who have been through the wringer alone and have never decompressed the way you have because they did not know about litigation stress. Be the solution!

You will likely have some "cleaning up" to do, as described elsewhere, narratives to write for the Board you are licensed under, reporting to credentialing organizations and payers. Look at each of these activities not as one more reminder but as one more step further away from the past. A change in thinking can bring about a change in attitude. Put differently: fake it until you can make it.

Finally, I have had some simple rules that I have tried to live by. I have not always succeeded, but fortunately I learned early on that in most areas of life you should seek excellence, not perfection. One rule is "Do the right thing for the right reason." This should need no explanation, but I learned early on that if I do that I can sleep at night and also look my kids in the eye...look anyone in the eye...and defend myself and my actions.

Another simple rule I pulled out of the movement back in the 1990s of Continuous Quality Improvement. The Japanese have a concept called **Kaizan.** It is really quite simple: live your life in such a way that you finish each day somehow better than you started it. I used it when I coached, when I taught, and in my professional life: finish this practice somehow better than you are starting it. Leave this class today somehow better than when you walked in here. Read one article that teaches you something new. It does not have to be huge, it does not have to be earth-shaking, just some sort of improvement.

And that is what I ask you to do when everything is over, find a way to focus on ending each day somehow better than when you started it. Is there an ulterior motive to this? Yes. If you are focused on Kaizan, what are you not focused on?

8. SUMMARY

Reviewing all that has been discussed, I explained to you the difference between stress, stressor, distress and eustress, all part of Hans Selye's General Adaption Syndrome, so that you have a grasp of the evolution of what most people today lump into the category of "suffering from stress." I also explained why you, as a health care provider, are particularly susceptible to extreme distress caused by a malpractice claim or litigation, what has come to be known as litigation stress. I hope the message I tried to convey was the message you received: **what you are experiencing is not only normal, but expected and that includes, in many cases, having an extreme response.**

In the process of explaining this to you I tried to emphasize that what was once a very useful bodily response, the "fight or flight" mechanism that helped keep our ancestors alive when every day they likely had to deal with at least one situation where their only two options were to fight or run away, if they wished to survive, is still with us. When faced with a threat today...or what you perceive as a threat...your brain still elicits the same fight or flight response: blood flow is directed towards muscles that can move you, skeletal muscles, and away from muscles superfluous to fighting or fleeing, internal muscles or involuntary muscles. Organs necessary to either fight or run away, specifically you heart and brain, get filled with blood and chemicals of action, while organs that are either unnecessary or even counterproductive, such as your stomach, receive a reduced blood flow. This is, as a reminder, why getting stress levels under control, being able to dial it down from distress to manageable stress, is important to your long-term health; continued disruption of normal blood flow to internal organs and the increase in the chemicals of stress over a long period of time can have a deleterious impact on your health.

The key point is that over the centuries little has changed in the fight or flight mechanism, it is the "threats" we must deal with today that have largely changed. What we often perceive as a threat today are not things we can readily fight or run away from. Your body is geared up for action, to fight or flee, while your mind tells you to stop, it tells you that at the very least the lesser of the two evils is to run away…which often leaves you stewing in the juices of stress. Your gas pedal and brake pedal are both stuck to the floor.

A quick example. I took a break from writing this section to drive up to the store. I wanted to pick up some donuts to have with my glass of Slim Fast. Just kidding, we needed eggs and cream. But I digress. I was at an intersection that had two left-turn lanes with dashed lines to remind drivers to stay in whichever lane they started in: if you started in the left-hand left-turn lane, turn into the left lane of the road; if you started in the right-hand left-turn lane you should turn into the right lane. Or, in other words, stay in your own lane when turning. Pretty simple, correct?

Yet as I turned from the right-side left-turn lane into the right lane, staying in my lane, the "gentleman" in the vehicle next to mine made his turn from the left-hand turning lane into the right lane, basically driving somewhat diagonally across the turning lanes and forcing me to swerve into a merge lane coming from the other direction.

.

Fortunately there were no vehicles merging. In an attempt...make that stupid attempt...to bring the error of his driving habits to his attention, and to keep him from hitting me, I blew my horn at the other driver. Rather than the expected "I'm sorry, my bad!" wave I was greeted with a one-finger salute.

An accident almost happened. It was likely not going to be life threatening, but it was still an attack on my physical being. Fight or flee? Chase him all the way to the next county and confront him, or swallow the chemicals of stress? I swallowed, then performed belly-breathing until I parked the car in front of the grocery store. I will admit to keeping an eye open for him, more to brace myself for words directed at me by him, but I did not see him again.

In my younger days? We might still be driving with me following him until a convenient time to stop and have a "discussion."

This is a good example, a good reminder that these sorts of "fight or flight" opportunities are occurring to you every day. Every. Day. Stress is responding to the world around you. The first issue is your brain determining if something is a threat to your person; if the brain perceives it as a threat the fight or flight mechanism will kick in and you then have some decisions to make; please remember that peace is one of the choices.

In the section on Post-Traumatic Stress Disorder remember that it is the opinion of many that we have an entire country, perhaps an entire world, walking around with at least a low level of PTSD brought on by all of the events of the last 20-30 years, from the World Trade Center bombing to the hyper-partisanship in our political system brought about primarily by gerrymandering, lobbyists and consultants, to the events of 09/11/2001, to the global economic meltdown that resulted in the perpetrators of the meltdown being left rich, very rich, richer than the bottom 99% of the U.S. population. While millions of people lost jobs, life savings, homes, and in America access to health insurance, the people who caused it assumed an Alfred E. Neuman look from Mad Magazine and asked, "Who? Me?" The major difference between this day-in and day-out stress and litigation stress is the magnitude of your response, the longevity of the event, the up-and-down emotions and time commitment of the event, and the challenge that once it's over, it isn't over. In fact, for as long as you practice it will never be completely over, but with time the stress response will fade as the perceived threat to your career and reputation fade. But it never completely disappears. Just when you think the Fat Lady is getting ready to sing you figure out she has not even shown up at the theater, yet. Kaizan.

What did we try to accomplish?

- **Introduction:** I tried to communicate to you how it is that I came to be involved in the issue of litigation stress, how I have been writing about it and lecturing about it, my real-world experience in dealing with health care providers and in many cases dealing with them from the occurrence of the event until years after everything is allegedly over. As any medical professional will tell you, book learning is fine but nothing beats learning from experience. It may be a difficult teacher, in that it gives you the test, then teaches you the lesson, but experience is a great teacher.

- **Chapter 1. What is malpractice and who is to blame?** If I have to distill this entire chapter down to one word, it would be "humans." We are the reason. We are the patient, the health care provider, the plaintiff's attorney, the defense attorney...we are all humans and that is the one and only constant. If somehow the filing of a medical malpractice claim was declared illegal tomorrow, a Constitutional amendment was put on the books that medical malpractice injuries were not compensable and that no physician, dentist, nurse practitioner, physician assistant, dental hygienist, that no health care professional could be sued for malpractice, would malpractice stop? Would no more bad outcomes occur? Would health care costs decrease? Would health care providers practice better medicine? The answer to all of the preceding questions is "no" and, thus, humans are to blame for malpractice. We are not perfect.

- **Chapter 2. Stress and Litigation Stress.** For some this may have seemed dry and boring, for others it was a good refresher or reminder. In other cases you may have been exposed to these concepts for the first time. I often used to use the word "impacted" during lectures, until a gastroenterologist come up to me after one presentation and made two comments: first, he said all the information on stress and the

.

chemicals and reactions was new to him (in my mind a failing of our health care education system); and, the word "impacted" had an entirely different meaning to him than to most of the other attendees! Both excellent points! Hopefully, however, you came away with a better understanding of how we have remained the "victims" of our ancestral DNA for thousands of years after we have been said to have evolved. Stress in and of itself is not bad; prolonged high levels of stress or distress can eventually lead not only to physical problems but can set up a feedback loop where each stressful event is piled on top of the ones before until the layers become too much to deal with at one time, so they must be peeled back like an onion, one layer at a time.

Chapter 3. Litigation Stress in health care professionals. In this chapter we worked at trying to get you to understand how almost everything about you as a person, how you were trained as a health care professional, about how you work at your profession every day and the impact all of this has had on your ability to separate who you are from what you do makes you susceptible to an over-reaction to litigation, to litigation stress. Some of the very traits that help you be successful at what you do also set you up for having a severe emotional reaction if someone comes to you and says, in effect, "I was injured and it is your fault." At the same time that I tried to encourage you to work at separating who you are from what you do I was also trying to help you

.

understand that even if a person was injured, even if a person did not improve, even if a person did not have a good outcome, it does not automatically mean that you committed malpractice. You may have achieved the best outcome anyone could have achieved and it just did not meet the patient's expectations (or the patient's family's expectations) and they feel they need to be made whole. This, too, we can blame on our DNA as going back to Biblical times the desire to be made even or whole in the face of a loss was documented. If your tribe killed one of my sons, I was essentially empowered to kill one of your sons and we were even, let's get on with survival. If, however, I killed two of your sons in retaliation for the killing of one of my sons, we were not even, I was "ahead" and you had the right, even the expectation, to be made even, to be made whole. The whole basis of our legal system was supposed to be built around this ability to make things even, to make people whole, perhaps without killing involved, but as I noted the civil legal system today is not about good and bad, right and wrong, or making people whole by handing out justice (see "*The Myth of Moral Justice*" by Thane Rosenbaum as one of the resources in the bibliography at the end). The civil legal system has been perverted by the wealthy and the powerful, the corporations and the lobbyists, and this actually works to the advantage of you as a defendant in a civil case as the money is on your side. The Plaintiff has to be

209

.

perfect to get the case to a jury, then educate and convince the jury; the Defense, you, have money and expertise on your side, plus the respect the common person has for the health care profession. Thus in medical malpractice cases the defense wins in excess of 80% of the time, regardless of the insurance company or, in some cases, even the facts. It is a costly, time consuming, emotionally-draining experience and that is by design. If you want simple justice, quick and simple, watch "Judge Judy" on TV. No lawyers, just two parties with a dispute seeking a quick resolution. Not practical for a medical malpractice case? Likely not, as the Plaintiff would be at even more of a disadvantage than he/she is now. But with the occurrence-to-settlement lag time on average 4.9 years, it is difficult to argue that any justice was swift, nor was anything necessarily learned by the defendant after the passage of so much time. There are better ways to handle these disputes, but it would require each side giving up some leverage. Unless and until that occurs, understand that what you are feeling is normal, that any defendant in litigation experiences similar feelings, but your reaction may be more extreme.

Chapter 4. Post-Traumatic Stress Disorder. In this chapter I wanted to quickly take you through the change in thinking that has occurred over the last 30 years or so with PTSD. It is not just "in your head" but can actually change the way your brain functions. Nothing in this chapter was intended to denigrate the brave men and women of our armed forces and the PTSD that they must deal with after returning from combat. Nor was it intended to denigrate victims of violence, especially those people in war torn countries around the world or those living in neighborhoods right here in the United States where violence is a fact of daily life. What has changed is the understanding that people can suffer from PTSD without going to war or suffering through physical violence, that different people have different levels of susceptibility to PTSD whenever they are hit by a traumatic event, be it physical violence or emotional violence, such as the loss of a spouse, parent or child to death, a divorce or a job loss, especially a job loss that, during the Great Recession, resulted in the loss of homes, retirement income, any chance of finding a similar job at a similar salary level, little or no hope of rebuilding retirement funds, and gradually realizing that not only were specific people to blame for the Great Recession, but that these people were handsomely rewarded financially while the bottom 95% of us were forced to live in fear every day, even if we had jobs. Here you had someone who specifically caused this global disaster and who knew it was going to happen, they did it regardless, the government turned the other way, and the bottom 95% are still dealing with the lingering effects of this today. I personally know of people who lost positions in 2008 and 2009 who have never found a

211

comparable position or salary, to this day. Thus the opinion of many that as a country we have a large number of people who spend each day dealing with a low level of PTSD without knowing it. What research is trying to determine today is why multiple people, when exposed to the same trauma, can have responses from something very short-term and mild along a continuum to debilitating. What causes some people to be more resilient to bouncing back from a trauma that, for another person, changes his or her life forever, changes them as a person, perhaps leaves them on an emotional ledge ready to go off at any moment? If a past malpractice claim is the strongest predictor of a future malpractice claim, is PTSD the reason? Why do some people give up, while others arise each morning filled with optimism that today is the day things turn around? Knowledge before the fact can impact your resilience, can be a determining factor, and you now have this knowledge.

Chapter 5. Stress Management Techniques. After hopefully helping you understand why litigation occurs, explaining very briefly the etiology of the stress responses we have today and why litigation might cause a severe emotional reaction in you, then taking a brief detour into examining the role PTSD may play in all of this, I gave you tools, most of them fairly simple tools, to help you reduce the level of distress you may be dealing with to manageable levels. If lack of control or perceived lack of control is what causes

.

most of our severe stress and distress today, what can be done to treat the symptoms, to help protect us from the effects of long-term, chronic distress or litigation stress? You may have read about some of the steps you can take to deal with litigation sense and said to yourself, "These are all common sense." To a certain extent you are correct. One challenge, however, is consciously making the time and effort to engage in these activities when your mind is already not working correctly. That is where picking up this book can help as it will remind you of the things you need to do to regain control of your body. Left to your own devices you may simply stew in the juices of stress and not only harm your body, but also harm the defense of your claim, harm your relationships, and harm your career. Another thought on the "common sense" aspect of the stress management techniques is the belief by many that the most common thing about common sense is how uncommon it is. I think the quote might have come from Will Rogers or Mark Twain in a slightly different format, but you get the idea. Sometimes we know what needs to be done but stress prevents us from seeing it. This chapter essentially encourages you to treat yourself kindly, take care of yourself, put yourself first occasionally, and work at separating who you are from what you do.

⁜ Chapter 6: Post-Litigation

In this final chapter I ask you to do a few things, a little post-storm clean up. First, take some quiet

213

.

time and reflect in excruciating detail what happened and if there was anything you could have done differently that might have altered the outcome. Could you have taken alternative steps to have prevented the claim completely? Could you have communicated better with the patient or family? Did you miss something in the assessment? When things started going "south" did you try to ignore the situation instead of having an open an honest conversation with the patient or the family? Remember that often patients claim that the only way they could find out everything possible about their condition and care was to file a malpractice claim. I also recommended you take an assessment of yourself, mentally, physically and emotionally, to determine if you might benefit from some professional help or if you should consider continuing with your stress management activities, developed during the claim, to strengthen your resiliency for the future? As Mark Twain once said:

"A man with a tiger by the tail knows two or three things more than a man who has never had a tiger by the tail."

You are now, for better or worse, more knowledgeable about litigation, malpractice claims, stress, stress management, depositions, etc. than most other physicians: become a supportive colleague, especially if a colleague

.

supported you during your claim. You won't want to discuss facts, but everything else that occurred, the emotions, what your attorney said and did, what the plaintiff's attorney said and did, how this impacted your family, how this impacted your practice, all of this is fair game to discuss and help a fellow health care provider get through the process. This is especially important if you are a male, which means you are unlikely to have a strong social network; contemplate setting up or joining a support group or network where everyone, experienced or inexperienced, can discuss the process, the feelings, the roller coaster, the fear, the desire to strangle the plaintiff's attorney (that is likely misplaced anger, by the way), all aspects of dealing with a malpractice claim. One hour per week is not too much to give as a means of either paying it back or paying it forward, however you want to look at it. The key, if you can recall, is to make you whole again, physically and emotionally. I want you to be the same health care practitioner, spouse, friend, parent, and person that you were before the claim occurred…and maybe even better! Wouldn't that be something, for you to come out of a malpractice claim a better person than the one who went into it?

Because if you don't or can't move on, if the after-effects or PTSD or whatever you want to call it causes you to forever be stuck as the person you became during the claim, because of the claim, the likely outcome may be…

.

*Six humans trapped by happenstance in bleak
and bitter cold.*

**Thanks for all you do, I hope you found
something useful or beneficial in these
words, good luck and God bless!**

Epilogue

After researching stress management, teaching seminars on dealing with stress, developing seminars and lectures, plus a program on litigation stress in health care professionals, writing articles, after being deposed twice, once as a fact witness and once as an "expert" witness, after all the work and time put into helping others help themselves, I found myself in litigation for the first time in my life at the ripe old age of 59. It was a business dispute concocted by my then employer, totally false and with a twist worthy of a John Grisham novel. The initial law suit and allegations that were spread about me had nothing to do with the real reason the suit was filed (think about the original version of the move "*Wizard of Oz*" and at the end where the "wizard" implores Dorothy and friends to "Ignore that man behind the curtain!"). But while I cannot go into details here, nor are they necessary, the take away is essentially one of "*physician heal thyself.*" I did some things well, just as discussed in this book, and some other things I handled very badly.

Let me cut myself some slack here in the beginning: this was a business lawsuit, not a malpractice suit. The suit was filed by a business that uses the legal system as part of its business strategy, as many large companies do. Facts were present, as with a malpractice suit, but the attorneys for my former employer followed the course of action that all good corporate litigators follow:

1. If you have bad facts, argue the law.
2. If you have bad law, argue the facts.

217

.

3. If you have bad law and bad facts, change the story. (They could not as it was their story to begin with)
4. If you can't change the story, bang on the table! Attack either the plaintiff or the plaintiff's attorney, another way to change the story.

What is important to note in my case, beyond it being a business case and not a malpractice case, is that my former employer put in its initial complaint and its amended complaint that it wanted a jury trial, but not just any jury trial: it wanted an **expedited** jury trial, a jury trial held as soon as possible due to the egregious harm I was likely to cause the company, or so they argued. This was in February 2009. Six months after the law suit was filed they sent out nine subpoenas looking for evidence, but also as a means of letting people know that there was a lawsuit filed against me and no one can file a fake lawsuit, correct? As one attorney told me, sending out subpoenas, even if you don't expect to get anything useful in return, is a legal way to let people know that a lawsuit has been filed and plays into the belief that someone cannot file a fraudulent law suit. Just short of three years later they nonsuited the case without ever asking the court to set a trial date. Expedited jury trial? How about ANY jury trial?

I point this out to you only to illustrate how dissimilar civil proceedings can be, despite being governed by the same Rules of Civil Procedure. While there are similarities in proceedings, a medical malpractice proceeding usually comes down to dueling experts trying to convince the jury what the standard of care was and how it was or was not met. In a business case everyone,

218

judge, jury, attorneys, must all deal with facts and "alternative facts" and facts that are relevant or irrelevant, most designed to confuse the counsel for the other side, the judge, and/or the jury. Having now seen it up close it is not pretty. I was forced to read and listen to things said about me that were flat out lies and other things that were misrepresentations, words taken out of context. Rumor, innuendo, and out of context messages, emails and comments, have no place in a true fact-finding mission. The key to obtaining facts and ascertaining the truth begins with full transparency, not selective messaging. Early on in a malpractice case the same thing may happen to you.

As the case started and I saw things in print that were not only untrue but easily proven to be untrue, I will admit to being astounded. You may have the same feeling when you first read the pleading in a malpractice case against you. I remember asking my attorney how someone could state these things in a pleading to the court that are not only lies, but easily proven to be lies? His response was that where there is usually a big firm, big money and insurance money, they can say whatever they want to in order to inflame the senses of the court and…remember this part…get under your skin. In the filing they can say anything; they will not have to actually prove anything unless and until the case gets to a jury. This is one reason why so many cases never get to a jury; the plan of the defense from the beginning, given that in corporate law the defense is usually defending that which is indefensible (unless you have two really big companies going at it and then it likely will be a case of who is the least guilty) is to beat the plaintiff up, drag the case on

219

with continuances, and keep it going so long the plaintiff eventually gives up and takes whatever is offered.

Or as my one attorney put it, being dragged nekkid through the briar patch. This is a business case. This is a case where one side uses the civil legal system to achieve a business goal.

This will likely **not** be your case, but I wanted to set up some of the differences ahead of time so what I am about to tell you is more understandable.

Discovery

Your discovery process will mostly be to ascertain facts pertinent to your case, the Standard of Care mentioned earlier. You will be asked about your education, training, experience, previous claims, and the like. You will be asked about records and documents.

By contrast, my former employer went through five law firms and 18 attorneys, and as part of the discovery process they each asked for the same documents, over and over. The goal: find one batch of documents that is missing something that was part of a previous batch of documents, solely to paint me as devious, deceitful, untruthful, and the like. Relevant? Immaterial. This will become a more important tactic in malpractice cases due to the use of electronic medical records, the Internet of Things, and the long electronic trail that will be out there for you, your patient, your partners, everyone. Tread carefully.

As noted I am not a fan of electronic medical records, as I think they impede good physician-patient communication, guide you towards boxes to check that will increase reimbursement (which will one day likely be

220

considered fraud), and in general simply help payers determine who they want to keep and who is an "outlier." The one aspect of electronic medical records that I think will be helpful is that they will decrease negative comments getting into the record, something we always cautioned providers about when writing or dictating a record. One of the more difficult comments to defend when a bad outcome turned into a malpractice suit was the comment a physician made that a patient was "...*in need of high-speed lead therapy*." In other words, she was a difficult patient who needed to be shot. Not a pertinent part of the note and one your defense attorney might get thrown out as irrelevant, but the use of electronic records can decrease comments such as these from getting into the record.

Similarly we once had a close call that might have turned on documentation that was thorough, timely, accurate...and would have killed the doctor at trial. When a hospitalized patient took a turn for the worse the charge nurse attempted to contact the patient's physician, was unsuccessful, and documented it. She tried six more times during the shift to contact the physician, was unsuccessful, and documented the record each time. Except at the end of the last statement, before the change of shift, she added "...*unable to once again reach physician, probably shacked up with girlfriend for the weekend*." Accurate? Unfortunately very accurate. Relevant? Up to a point as there were also on-call physicians available, but the admitting physician had left instructions to be contacted if the patient took a turn for the worse. The on-call was eventually summoned and dealt with the situation. The documentation only became

221

an issue because the on-call physician noted it and brought it to the attention of the hospital risk manager.

But at least it was well-documented. And it was accurate!

Interrogatories

These will be the questions you are asked leading up to the depositions. Your attorney will instruct you to answer each one as thoroughly and accurately as possible, but not to volunteer information. You will send the answers to your attorney who will review them with you and edit them as necessary. You will want to keep a copy for your own records to review them the night before your deposition, as most of the questions in the interrogatories will be asked in the deposition. I was fine with those questions because they actually dealt with the case in some way.

Depositions

This is where I lost it! Way back in Chapter 3 I talked about depositions, and how and why they are important. They are the best way for you to present yourself as a solid, credible witness on your own behalf. In my case I did not do well and here is what happened. I offer myself as an example of what you should <u>not</u> do!

Just prior to my deposition the defense attorneys (3) scheduled my daughter and wife to be deposed. I will tell you that if that type of scheduling occurs in your case <u>tell your attorney to change it</u>! Both my daughter and wife were listed as potential witnesses solely to discuss the emotional and financial impact on the family, based on what my former employer had done. Instead my <u>daughter</u>

spent 45 minutes being asked question after question about school, grades, an email she had inadvertently sent to my old work email address talking about how angry she was over my firing, which the defense attorney attempted to use to demonstrate my daughter was unstable (she had, by the way, been forced to drop out of college in her last semester because of my termination by my former employer).

My wife spent close to an hour and one-half answering question after question about the business and business dealings of a former business partner, each question completely unrelated to my case. As my wife was repeatedly forced to answer, "I don't know" to question after question, the defense attorney feigned disgust and insinuated she was conveniently forgetting answers, while the president of the company that had fired me sat off to the side laughing. In all honesty I could not have answered the questions.

You are thinking that this cannot be right, that this cannot be acceptable behavior in our legal system. If you read through Bar Association ethics manuals, national or state, it is not acceptable. But lawyers are loathed to report each other for misconduct and judges are loathed to hand down sanctions for this sort of "Rambo lawyering." However, the key point I want you to remember is this: the depositions of my daughter and wife, performed just ahead of my deposition, were not done for gathering useful information for either my case against my former employer or their counter-claim against me. As my former employer had already lost a companion case in a jury trial it had already made the decision to settle. The issue was how to get the settlement as low as possible. One way

223

was to try to manipulate me into giving a bad deposition and, unfortunately, it worked.

By the time we walked into a separate room for my deposition I was steaming mad over the treatment of my wife and daughter. Since meeting her I have repeatedly had people tell me that my wife is the nicest person they have ever met or known. Yet after her deposition she used language to describe the defense attorney that no one had heard her use before. At that point I should have requested the deposition be held on another day, feigned illness or something because I was angry. I did not want to give a deposition, I wanted to take the defense attorney out in the alley! This is not the right frame of mind for a deposition.

My deposition was also different in that it was recorded, but not everyone: just me. I had a camera stuck about 18" from my face and was told to sit perfectly still so that I stayed in frame; I was not allowed to move around at all. Meanwhile everyone else could move around, go in and out of the room, employees came and went, got coffee and sodas, while I had to sit up straight and still, and then was put through the same drill as my wife and daughter: question after question unrelated to either case. At one point the corporate defense attorney asked me a question for which I did not know the answer, but my former employer did. It had to do with what my former employer called the "total blow up plan" to provoke me into quitting. When the corporate defense attorney asked the question he then turned his back to me and faced the opposite wall!

Despite all that I have written here, despite years of talking about this and writing about this and conducting

224

seminars about this, **I lost it**. I refused to answer. When the defense attorney, still facing the opposite wall, asked the question again I told him I would not answer until he turned around and faced me, looked at me, that I was not going to talk to his back.

At that point the defense attorney instructed my attorney to call for a recess so that my attorney could *"...get your client under control."*

My attorney did call for a recess and pulled me aside and read me the riot act. I told him I had been sitting for, at that point six hours of a deposition with only one or two questions related to either case. He admonished me that most of these questions would be tossed out as being irrelevant, which is why he was objecting to every question, and he was correct.

THEREFORE, take all I have said about depositions to heart, prepare for them, have your defense team conduct mock depositions if necessary, but if you are recorded, if a camera is stuck in front of your face and your face only, as soon as you are asked the first question, which will be to state your name, I want you to state also the following:

"My name is _____ and I want anyone viewing this deposition to be aware of the circumstances of this deposition. There is a camera 18" from my face. No one else is having their face recorded. People will be leaving and entering the room, moving about, while I am forced to sit completely still for however long this deposition lasts. If anyone on the opposing side does anything to provoke me or behaves in an irritating or agitating manner I will point it out to you before, during, or after

my answer to any question. And if any portion of this deposition is used in court I insist that this introduction be shown to the jury so the jury understands the circumstances of this deposition. If opposing counsel does not agree to show this portion of the recording then I refuse to be recorded and this deposition is over."

Sounds crazy, right? It's not. While the intention is to use these Rambo-like interrogation tactics, you have a right to be treated civilly and as a human being. A deposition is a part of the discovery process and, as such, it is supposed to be used to learn factual information directly related to the case or cases at hand. Anything beyond that is supposed to be unethical.

You are likely asking how this is allowed to go on? Two reasons. First, lawyers used to be considered Officers of the Court and, as such, had their first responsibility to the court, to the facts, to the truth. While still considered Officers of the Court, their role has evolved into aggressively representing their client in any way possible and at any cost possible, with little or no thought given to the court, facts, sanctions, or anything else. As Al Davis, the owner and sometime coach of the Oakland Raiders used to tell his players, "*Just win, baby*."

The second reason it is allowed to go on is because there is a pecking order that exists, deservedly or not. The assumption is that a lawyer with a big firm is a better lawyer than one with a small firm or, heaven forbid, a solo practitioner. In addition, who is a judge, consciously or unconsciously, going to rule against, the lawyer who is in his courtroom on a regular basis and who he also likely sees at the local country club each weekend, the lawyer whose children likely go to the same school as the judge's children or grandchildren? Or, is the judge more likely to rule in favor of a lawyer in a small practice or in solo practice who argues brilliantly, is spot on for every issue of law and every fact, and who has met every filing deadline...but the judge likely won't see this lawyer again for a long time?

Am I suggesting a rigged system? Corruption? Not consciously, not maliciously. But a tilted playing field? Well, I know in my case I read rulings handed down by two judges that had multiple errors of fact, yet the ruling went against me. On one issue I remember thinking that the judge must have read a completely different document than the one in my case, then wrote his opinion. The facts he cited were almost the polar opposite of what were in my case.

Lesson? Control. Gain as much control over the situation as possible to reduce your distress. There are facts, to be sure, but whereas one side (me) was trying to get the facts before a jury, the other side was doing all it could to prevent a jury trial while trying to change the story, trying to pull a "Wizard of Oz" defense where they wanted the jury to ignore the facts and, instead, listen to the story that was being created by the defense. Will the jury believe the story made up by the defense or their own lying eyes?

Be prepared for the deposition, factually and emotionally, and keep your emotions under check. Your attorney and claims manager should try to help you with this, but it is where my case was greatly weakened; I walked into the deposition looking for a fight because of

227

the way my wife and daughter had been treated, rather than walking in sure of my facts and ready to answer any question as truthfully and honestly as possible, regardless of any antics by the opposing lawyer to provoke me.
I had met the enemy and it was me!

Meta Data Searches

This is something new that is either a great benefit to the truly good and clean person in a law suit or the Devil walking the earth. Much has been written in recent years about email and the role it has come to play in court proceedings, civil and criminal. Now this has been expanded to include the Internet of Things, as every computerized device is in some way linked to every other computerized device and keeps a record of what it has done. Sometimes what is found is blatant, but most of the time one side will intentionally misinterpret something that was written to gain an advantage.

More importantly in some cases, it is what is not found in the email or other evidence that can cause a problem for one side of the other, and this is where meta data searches are either used or misused by one side or the other. If you have never heard this before, hear it now: when something is typed into a computer it is forever or as close to forever as something can get. Yet the bad news for the good guys is that recent court decisions have found that if something is missing or can't be found, then it is missing or can't be found, no fault. My bad.

A meta data search takes a picture of the hard drive of your computer, tablet, smart phone, lap top, etc., and can then pull up everything that was ever typed, sent, viewed,

.

a complete record. Normally courts do not favor meta data searches because of the increased opportunity for mischief ("*Ladies and gentlemen of the jury, he may claim to be a good physician but he looks at pornography on his computer!*). Now, let's say the preceding is exactly what happens: is it relevant to the case? Certainly not in a medical malpractice case, but you can see the opportunity for mischief, to try to taint the jury. And your defense attorney would certainly try to get something such as that not allowed into evidence as it certainly is irrelevant, but you never know how a lawyer will argue or a judge rule. And how is a jury supposed to "forget" what it heard? Thus, one complaint about meta data searches.

Another complaint is what happens if there are incomplete or missing files: was it a deliberate attempt to mislead or someone simply trying to keep a computer from getting too clogged up with stuff? My attorney told me never delete anything; another attorney, a friend of mine, told me when we were on the phone that he was about to delete 257 emails with one key stroke. The conflict arises between what is relevant and what is irrelevant, but also if something is missing it allows one side to paint the other as being dishonest and hiding evidence.

In my case I was subpoenaed once by two of the first three law firms involved to turn over all documents within certain parameters and on certain subjects. I complied to the best of my ability to do so. Then my former employer changed law firms, same questions asked, same search conducted, and to the best of my ability the same documents sent. Then my former employer changed firms again, went to law firm #5, and they asked for the same documents that had already been asked for twice. I asked my attorney if these law firms, when the case was moved from one firm to another, did not get the material from the preceding firm or firms and simply review it, and the answer was that the defense firms make money by billing either the client or the insurance company for the client, so financially it is in their best interest to just keep starting over. Plus, it gives the last firm on the case one possible advantage and it occurred in my case.

When the last requests came in for documents it was over three years after I had been terminated and my employer filed its lawsuit against me, since dropped. Understand that not only do courts not like metadata searches but when they are favored is close to the time of the event, to "freeze" the record at the time things are happening. Does this sound like medical record documentation? It is the same concept. Because two things can happen over a two or three-year period: first, emails can get lost, deleted, damaged, and conversations can occur that the person sending or receiving the email believes to be innocuous; and, second, in reproducing documents over and over, especially if you assume the documents are being passed from law firm to law firm, you may turn over a document in response to one request and then not turn it over in response to a similar, but not identical, request. Harken back to my experience with the defense attorney asking two similar, but not identical, questions which elicited two different answers.

In my case emails were not sent in response to the third request, based on the wording, and emails were found in the meta data search that I did not think were pertinent or relevant (so I either had not sent them or I deleted them) but the other side did (or claimed to, for the sake of painting me as dishonest and to gain a second trial continuance). But these emails in question had nothing to do with what was happening around the time of and immediately after I was fired, they were sent months or years later. In one case my former employer released an email chain from 2002, before I was even their employee, that they had taken off of my computer when all the data was transferred to their computers in 2006. In 2012 they brought up this 2002 email to try and prove I already had a bad reputation and, thus, anything they said or did could not ruin my reputation. Ironically this email chain was a debate between me and the General Counsel for an insurance company that, to make a long story short, I won and he apologized for...which my former employer conveniently forgot to include. But this is a great example of why courts, for the sake of relevance, favor meta data done at or near the time of the event.

Lesson? Use the telephone. Seriously. Say it, forget it; write it, regret it.

What does this have to do with the civil procedure and the facts that are supposed to decide the case? Usually absolutely nothing, it is all just part of the game. As I said, the legal system is about the legal system, it is not about the law, not about right and wrong, not about good and bad, unless and until you get in front of a jury, and that happens only about 3% to 5% of the time.

231

Bibliography/Resources

The author acknowledges that many of his ideas, strategies and opinions came from life, teachers, friends and, most importantly, members of the health care community with whom he has dealt these past 25 years. But ideas and thoughts also came from reading the following books and every effort has been made to give credit for direct quotes. If any direct quote has not been properly attributed it is solely the fault of the author, for which he apologizes.

Babiak, Paul, Ph.D., & Hare, Robert D., Ph.D. *Snakes in Suits: When psychopaths go to work.* New York: Harper Collins, 2006

Charles, Sara, MD, Frisch, Paul R., JD. *Adverse Events, Stress, and Litigation.* New York: Oxford University Press, 2005.

Charles, Sara, MD; Kennedy, Eugene. *Defendant, a psychiatrist on trial for medical malpractice: an episode in America's hidden health care crisis.* New York: Free Press, 1985.

Edlund, Matthew, M.D. *The Power of Rest: Why sleep alone is not enough.* New York: Harper Collins e-books, 2010

Eliot, Robert S.; MD, Breo, Dennis L. *Is it worth dying for?* New York: Bantam Books, 1984

Gladwell, Malcolm. *David and Goliath: Underdogs, Misfits, and the Art of Battling Giants.* New York: Little Brown and Company, 2013

Goleman, Daniel. *Emotional Intelligence.* New York: Bantam Books, 1995.

McGraw, Phillip C., Ph.D*., Life Code: The New Rules for Winning in the Real World.* Los Angeles: Bird Street Books, 2009

Posner, Richard A. *How Judges Think.* Cambridge: First Harvard University Press, 2008

Rosenbaum, Thane, JD. *Payback: The case for revenge.* Chicago: The University of Chicago Press, 2013.

Rosenbaum, Thane, JD. *The Myth of Moral Justice.* New York: HarperCollins, 2011

Stewart, James B., *Tangled Webs; How false statements are undermining America, from Martha Stewart to Bernie Madoff.* New York: The Penguin Press, 2011

Turow, Scott. *One L.* New York: Farrar, Straus and Giroux, 2010

About the Author

Thomas P. Cox has been (deep breath): a steel factory worker; waiter; teacher; coach; health educator; training & education coordinator and risk manager for a large medical center; claim adjuster for a surplus lines insurance company; claim manager for a medical malpractice insurance company; field underwriter, marketing representative, and risk manager for a medical professional liability company; a physician and hospital risk manager for a medical professional liability insurance company; and today is an independent insurance agent. Correct: he never could quite figure out what he wanted to be when he grew up. He has authored articles for various publications including: T*he Newsletter of the Harvard Medical Institutions; Journal of Humanistic Education; Virginia Dental Journal; Virginia Medical Quarterly; Journal of the American Society for Healthcare Risk Management; Athletic Journal;* and *Scholastic Coach.* He also was a contributing writer for *MD Magazine* and writes a monthly newsletter.

A son of the Midwest, Cox was born in Chicago (Go White Sox!) and was raised in the western suburbs. He lives in Virginia. He is married, has three children and two step-sons, one grandson, three step-grandsons, and two step-granddaughters. Of course, the grandkids don't know anything, so let's just say he has six grandchildren!   He has no pets.

.

236